Prosperous, Safe and Tax-Free

DEMYSTIFYING INDEX UNIVERSAL LIFE
One of the Best and Most Misunderstood
Financial Tools

Prosperous, Safe and Tax-Free

DEMYSTIFYING INDEX UNIVERSAL LIFE
One of the Best and Most Misunderstood
Financial Tools

ISBN 978-0-9762806-4-4
Printed in the USA

By ASD Publishing

This publication is designed to provide accurate and authoritative information in regard to the subject matter covered. It is offered with the understanding that neither the publisher nor the author is engaged in rendering legal, accounting, or other professional services. If legal advice or other expert assistance is required, the services of a competent professional person should be sought.

"Life Insurance is the only tool that takes pennies
and guarantees dollars."

— Ben Feldman

"A policy of life insurance is the cheapest and safest mode
of making a certain provision for one's family."

— Benjamin Franklin

When you transition from work to retirement,
your entire life changes,
especially your finances.

You are no longer contributing to your savings;
you are now withdrawing.

When you reach retirement,
you need to think differently
about your money.

Your financial goals should shift
from accumulation with risk,
to protection and income.

— D. Scott Kenik

Table of Contents

PART 1
People Like You

1   Why This Book is for You

Retirement means you no longer have to work—or at least "go to work" every day for a paycheck. The idea is you have made enough and saved enough money to be able to live comfortably when you are no longer working.

The game is to earn as much money as you can on the money that you have saved while you are working so that you have the income you need when you retire.

Pretty much everyone thinks "stock market" to make the money. The stock market can deliver spectacular returns. It can also devastate a portfolio when it crashes and you lose that money you have so carefully saved. It's not just "on paper." It's real money. If you had $100,000 in an account, the market falls 20%, and you wanted to withdraw your money, you would only have $80,000.

The second problem is that "income" issue. The "usual" retirement methods aren't always going to produce the income you need to live—the dividends on the stocks you have in your portfolio, for example.

When you are nearing retirement or are fully retired, you don't have the luxury to lose money.

What I'm about to show you is a safe, sound, and pretty amazing financial tool that you can use in retirement that gives you that income you need, tax-free if you want (*Who LOVES paying taxes? I've yet to meet that person*), and you can have money set aside for whatever you need or want: paying for college, weddings, toys, paying for your old age, or for that legacy you've always wanted to leave your grandkids.

Interested?

2 What This Book Is and Is Not

Rather than waiting until the end of this book to thank you for reading it, I am offering my gratitude upfront, because when people hear the words "life insurance," all too often they say to themselves, *"I don't want to think about life insurance. I don't want to hear about life insurance. I don't want life insurance."*

The good news is that this life insurance book is **not** about life insurance—not in the way you think about it, anyway.

This book is about one of the most effective, safest, prosperous, and best tools in the financial industry. It is about what no one wants to hear about, but what everyone needs to know.

Why?

Because this information can be life-changing to your financial well-being.

The first thing that you need to know is that there are several different types of life insurance and they each have their own benefits and purposes. The primary purpose of this life insurance book (*which is NOT about life insurance*) is to uncover, explore, demystify, and explain the financial wonder that is *Indexed Universal Life Insurance* (IUL).

But…but…but, you said this book was not about life insurance.

Correct, I did. This book is about how to:
- get tax-free income
- gain prosperous returns
- get protection against stock market crashes
- earn interest on money that you borrow instead of paying interest
- all by using the unique features of a specialized form of life insurance.

And, of course, you get the added advantage of a death benefit.

In other words, this book is about how to take advantage of the **unique financial and tax benefits of life insurance** that are not available in *any* other financial tool.

Get ready for the financial ride of your life.

Oh, and thanks in advance for reading it.

3   Types of Life Insurance

Let's start with the various types of life insurance so you can better understand their purposes and best use.

The two prime categories of life insurance are temporary and permanent.

Temporary or "Term" Life Insurance

Term insurance is temporary life insurance. It offers a specific death benefit for a specified number of years, or "term." Typically, term insurance is offered for ten to thirty years. The insurance contract ends at the end of its term; hence, it is temporary.

The purpose of term insurance is the death benefit. The death benefit is what makes it "insurance," and term is considered pure insurance—nothing added. Term insurance is what many call "your grandfather's life insurance," because for hundreds of years, term life insurance was the only kind of life insurance available.

Term insurance has no cash value and therefore cannot be used for wealth building or tax planning strategies. This is why I rarely recommend term life insurance.

However, this death benefit issue is important, and this is what you need to know:

The death benefit can be
- *level*, which means that it stays the same;
- *reducing*, which means that it lowers over time; or
- *increasing*, which means that the death benefit can increase in value over time.

Term insurance is typically purchased to replace the income of the insured to help the remaining family financially.

The death benefit that is paid out to the named beneficiary in a term policy comes income-tax free. It can be used for various purposes such as to purchase an annuity that pays a lifetime income. Or it can be purchased for a specific purpose such as paying for college for the kids or paying off the mortgage. It can be used for any reason.

There is even a special kind of term insurance designed specifically for paying off mortgages, often referred to as mortgage protection insurance. It is term insurance with a *reducing* death benefit. Designed to reduce the death benefit to keep pace with the reducing mortgage principle as it is lowered over time, mortgage protection insurance costs less than a level or increasing death benefit policy.

A term policy with an *increasing death benefit* is designed to start with a low death benefit to keep costs low. The amount of the death benefit increases over time as the insured's needs increase with higher income and debt. With an *increased* death benefit, the cost of the policy increases over time as well.

You can buy policies with low death benefits, such as burial polices, or with high benefits, even in the millions.

Once term insurance ends, the insured (the person or entities on which the death benefit is purchased), can choose to renew the policy or let it lapse. That decision is completely up to the insured.

The cost of term insurance is primarily based on the applicant's age, health, and length of term, but other factors such as driving record, type of employment, and credit score do factor in as well as other conditions.

Term insurance is the least expensive type of insurance; however, since a large portion of the cost calculation is based on age, renewal rates will rise, and can rise significantly. If your policy is a ten-year term starting at age twenty-five, the increase may not be that much at the renewal age of thirty-five. But if a twenty-year policy ends at age sixty-five, the increase in cost could be significant and even be possibly unaffordable.

For this reason, if just having the death benefit is important to you, you would be better off buying a policy that has a longer term rather than a shorter term with plans to renew.

However, there is a far better option for long-term coverage, one that allows you to build cash value in the policy, which gives you far more advantages than simply having the death benefit.

Permanent Cash-Value Life Insurance
The two main types of permanent cash-value life insurance are Whole Life and Universal Life. The latter has a special off-shoot called "Indexed Universal Life."

Permanent cash-value life insurance is designed to last your "whole" life. This is why it is called "permanent." This type of insurance does not expire unless you stop making your premium payments. Don't take the name too literally though, as it can be canceled if desired.

Permanent insurance combines the death benefit (the insurance portion) with a savings component. That's the "cash value" part that makes this type of insurance so valuable. The policy owner can withdraw from that cash value or borrow against it. Taxes will be due on the interest earned on any money withdrawn; however, money that is borrowed is tax-free.

This "tax-free" money borrowed against the life insurance policy is what makes it so special.

As with term life insurance, the death benefit is tax-free to the heirs. When you take a loan from your permanent insurance, the death benefit is basically used as collateral. Since the death benefit is tax-free, the loan proceeds are tax-free. You do not need to repay these loans; they can be paid off with the death benefit upon your passing. This can be a **huge** benefit as you will see in upcoming chapters.

To build cash value, the owner contributes more than the premium cost for the life insurance portion. All excess goes to the cash value account portion of the policy, which builds equity.

While Whole Life and Universal Life/Indexed Universal Life are all permanent cash-value life insurance, the policies do differ significantly.

Whole Life
Whole Life insurance has a fixed premium and death benefit, meaning that they do not change over the life of the policy. The cash accumulation portion of Whole Life offers a guaranteed interest rate plus a dividend.

Whole Life policies used to offer a guaranteed minimum interest rate of 4%. However, that was recently changed to a range of 2.5 to 4%. Dividends are not guaranteed. If issued, the amounts are determined by the individual life insurance company based on the returns of the company's investment portfolio, business expenses, and annual profits. Currently, most carriers are paying between 4.5% to 6.5% in interest rates and dividends. But again, that rate is not guaranteed. Only the minimum interest rate is. This type of policy is great for those who want to know exactly how much money they are going to make as a minimum.

It is important to note that the more your money is guaranteed to earn interest, the lower the interest rate is going to be. This is why Whole Life insurance never earns that much. It is a guaranteed rate of return. You can set your clock by its returns. Also, because the returns are guaranteed, it is more expensive to own than the other kind of permanent cash-value life insurance, the kind that I teased you with in the introduction.

Universal Life
Universal Life insurance is very flexible, meaning that the premium and death benefits can be changed. This offers significant advantages for both investment and inheritance considerations.

Universal Life used to offer a 3 to 3.5% minimum interest rate before the 2008 recession, but is now it closer to a 1% average. The overall returns are based on interest rates. Each insurance company decides which interest rates are used to determine the interest rates paid to policy holders. Often, Moody's Corporate Bond rate is used as a basis. Currently, annual rates seem to average 4.5 to 5% overall.

A variation of Universal Life is **Variable Universal Life**. This is a securities product, meaning that the investment portion of your premium is directly invested in the stock market. Because of this, only stock brokers and financial advisors charging a fee for their service can offer a Variable Life Insurance policy. Your earnings are based on the performance of the market. You can make money or you can lose money. There is risk with Variable Universal Life policies.

Because you can lose money, I don't recommend variable life insurance, especially for those nearing retirement or in retirement. Retirement requires safe money, money that you can't lose in the stock market.

Lastly, and *most* important, is the variant of Universal known as Indexed Universal Life (IUL), the most important and valuable kind of permanent cash-value life insurance.

There is a reason that IULs makes such a good financial tool: Indexed Universal Life credits your policy interest based on the performance on a stock market index. But here's the most important part, the primary difference between it and the others, if you will: Your money is not in the stock market. The index performance is used to determine your interest.

The higher the index performs, the higher your interest is credited. But, and this is a **HUGE** but, IULs have a zero floor which means that you can never lose money when the market crashes. **You participate in the upside of the market with none of the risk!**

The benefit of this is that long-term performance can average 10 to 15%.

You **never** lose money, and you can earn far more than a

guaranteed rate. There's a host of other benefits as well.

Sounds intriguing? Read on.

4   Who Uses IULs as Financial Tools?

The Wealthy

They say that the wealthy pay fewer taxes. Know why? Because they can afford to hire tax attorneys, estate planning attorneys, and tax planners who, among other things, advise them to use IULs to build their wealth, tax-free, and create lifetime, tax-free, income streams.

Why IULs? Because they are safe—there is no stock-market losses. But they also can give you stock-market-like returns. Those returns aren't quite as high as what's happening in the stock market, but the returns are competitive and, because of the death benefit portion of the policy, you can use it for tax-free income.

The attorneys and financial professionals who work for the wealthy are used to dealing with millions of dollars. But here's what's really amazing about IULs. The financial strategies are the same, no matter how many zeros you have on the amount you're putting into the policy.

That's what makes the IUL so important for financial planning—at any level. Including yours.

Top Corporations

Fortune 500 companies use IULs to give their executives tax-free income for life. It's a way to use what's called the "golden handcuffs." Work for the company for enough years (the handcuffs) and you will be paid tax-free income for life in retirement (the gold). These benefits can be in the form of annuities or Indexed Universal life.

Colleges

Do you know who the top-paid employees of the big colleges are? Most would say the President, but it's actually the coaches.

You don't often read about a coach's pay package, but here's an article about Michigan State Wolverines' head football coach, Jim Harbaugh. Harbaugh is a former NFL quarterback and his status as "legend" in college football is assured. His cash-value life insurance makes him football's top-paid coach.

November 16, 2016

Cash value life insurance makes Harbaugh college football's top-paid coach

This type of deferred compensation alternative appeals to talented leaders and executives

Michigan Wolverines head coach Jim Harbaugh watches during an NCAA college football game against the Maryland Terrapins in Ann Arbor, Mich., Saturday, Nov. 5, 2016. (AP Photo/Paul Sancya)

In November 2016, the news broke. The University of Michigan agreed to pay $2 million annually into a permanent cash-value life insurance policy. This effectively increased Harbaugh's pay to $7 million a year.

Most of the details of the deal were never released, but it was reported that Harbaugh is the owner of the policy and because of that, he can take withdrawals (taxed) or loans (income tax-free) from the policy.

The compensation strategy was designed so that Harbaugh would be provided with a projected $1.4 million dollars a year, starting at age 66 and continuing all the way through age

98. This essentially gives him millions of dollars of tax-free income during his retirement.[1, 2]

When an IUL policy is designed correctly, a person making far less than Harbaugh can still receive an income tax-free in retirement.

Banks

Banks use IULs. The legacy banks—Wells Fargo, Citi Corp, Bank of America—typically have $20+ billion parked in these plans. They often max out what the government will let them contribute. It's considered a liquid asset to them, which is a tier-one asset. It's like cash.

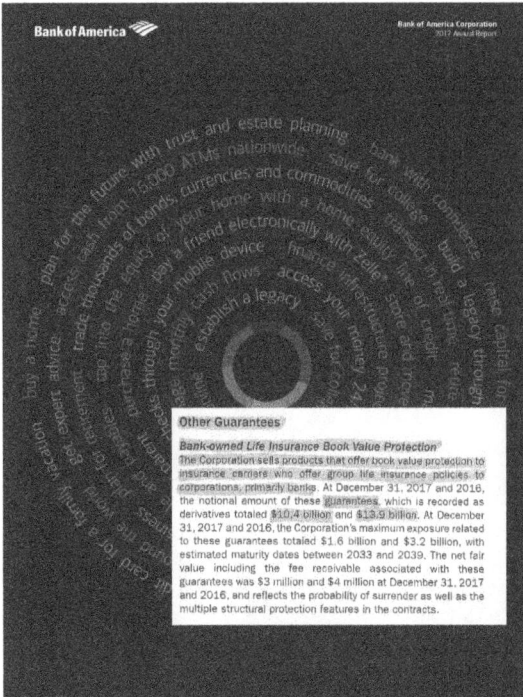

In 2017, according to their annual report, Bank of America had $24 billion in bank-owned life insurance. That staggering amount was categorized as "Other Guarantees." You read that correctly. Bank of America categorizes life insurance as "guaranteed." These policies are that safe.[3]

People Like You

Millions of Americans use permanent cash-value life insurance because of the benefits and advantages—competitive returns, safety, and tax-free income—remain the same no matter how much you have to put into the policy.

PART 2
What Makes IULs Such a
Great Financial Tool

5   Zero IS Your Hero

Here's what makes the IUL the best financial tool on the market.

The IUL has a zero floor.

What does this mean? That means the interest you earn in an IUL will **never** go below zero.

What does that mean?

You can **never lose** money.

That zero floor is one of the major advantages of Indexed Universal Life that I have been talking about. This *is* the guarantee.

When I tell people that with IULs, they will earn money when the index is positive, they love that.

But then when I tell them that when the stock market index goes negative, they won't earn any interest but they **won't lose any money**, for inexplicable reasons, some people become transfixed by the fact that they won't earn any interest when that happens.

They ignore the tremendous value of not losing money in down years.

Not losing money is the key feature, the best feature, it's one of the secret sauces of IULs. This is so much so that not earning interest in down years has earned the often-used moniker: **Zero Becomes Your Hero.**

The no-loss feature of Indexed Universal Life is what helps keep their performance high, long-term. Earning zero is far superior to losing.

Let's look at this chart which compares the performance of the S&P with a S&P Index with a 12.5% cap:

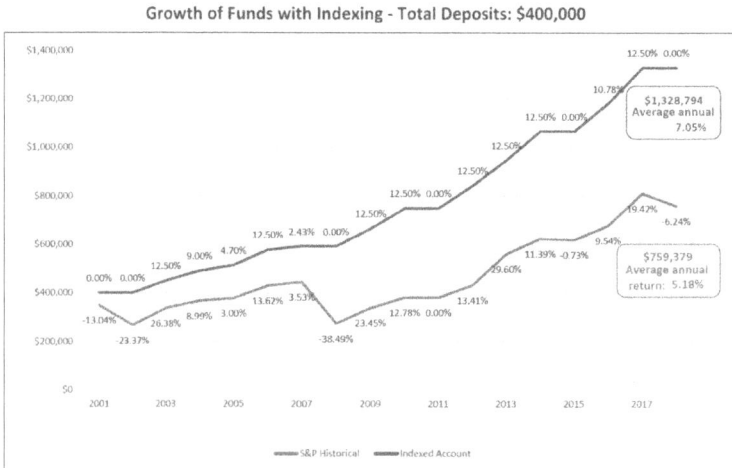

Growth of Funds with Indexing - Total Deposits: $400,000

Market returns assume S&P 500 Annual Returns Years 2001-2018, excluding dividends.
Indexed fund values do not include any costs.
Hypothetical example is for illustrative purposes only. This is not a prediction or guarantee of actual results, which will vary from those described.

© Scott Karstens does not provide tax, legal or accounting advice, nor is it designed - nor intended - to be applicable to any person's individual circumstances. This material has been prepared for information purposes only, and is not intended to provide, and should not be relied on for, tax, legal or accounting advice. You should consult your own qualified tax, legal and accounting advisors before engaging in any transaction.

Here's the same results in tabular form:

Year	S&P	Indexed
2002	-23.37	0.00
2003	26.38	12.50
2004	8.99	9.00
2005	3.00	4.70
2006	13.62	12.50
2007	3.53	2.43
2008	-38.49	0.00
2009	23.45	12.50
2010	12.78	12.50
2011	0.00	0.00
2012	13.41	12.50
2013	29.60	12.50
2014	11.39	12.50
2015	-0.73	0.00
2016	9.54	10.78
2017	19.42	12.50
2018	6.24	0.00
AVERAGE	**5.87**	**7.05**

With the zero floor and a 12.5% capped strategy, the impressive results above speak for themselves.

The difference in the average performance was only 1.18%, but it's the zero floor that makes the real difference. It's the "not losing" money difference. Over time the results are staggering. Just look at the two ending balances: $1.3 million versus $759k.

Zero *is* your hero.

6 Indexing

The **first** major secret sauce to the IUL is the zero floor.

The **second** is indexing. It's how your account gets credited with interest earned.

Indexing in a life insurance policy is not the same as "indexing" in the stock market environment.

A stock market index charts the performance of a certain group of stocks. A couple examples include:

- The S&P 500 index is the most well-known. It charts the performance of the top-producing 500 stocks.

- The Dow Jones Industrial is also an index. It's one of the oldest and most respected, and you often hear how the "Dow" performed on any given day.

Although the S&P and Dow are a couple of the most well-known, there are actually hundreds of indexes.

When you invest in an index fund like the S&P 500, your money is going directly into the stock market. If that stock market index doesn't do well in that year, then your returns are going to match what that index did. When the index loses money, that's what's going to happen to your money—you will lose money.

An index in an IUL is different and it works this way:
Your money isn't in the stock market or in an index fund,
but it uses an index, bonds, and options to determine your
interest. It makes stock-market-like gains, but doesn't lose
anything when the stock market falls below zero. It may
sound like a complicated process, but it's all done for you in
the background.

As I stated in the previously, life insurance index has a zero
floor. Even if the stock market crashes 19 percent, as it did in
2022, your IUL will *not lose* any money.

You decide which is better for your blood pressure.

Indexing Strategies
The index strategy for earning interest in your annuity can be
very lucrative. Indexing in insurance products started in 1995
with annuities. It was a way to provide annuity clients with
interest credited to their annuity that was above the standard
minimum guarantee of the annuity contract. It was done as
a way to help investors who were weary of the stock market
because it was fluctuating so wildly.

Two years later, the Indexed Universal Life policy was created,
and now over forty carriers use their version of this versatile
financial tool.

Indexing in life insurance was a strategy that caught on very
quickly because of the fact that you are guaranteed not to lose
any money while at the same time, you could earn more than
a fixed interest rate.

Picking an Index
With an Indexed Universal Life policy, you will have a choice
of various indexes from which to choose. The question

then becomes, how to pick one. Since none of us have a magical crystal ball to predict the future, we only have past performance to guide us.

In an indexed Universal Life Insurance policy, you will have a choice of various indices which are used to determine the amount of interest that you will be credited. You need to work with your financial professional closely on this issue because a trained agent will help you understand how to read an IUL illustration.

You will learn more about IUL illustrations in a later chapter, but for now, know that your choice of indices will be listed on that illustration and it will also provide historical performance data. Look at both the short- and long-term performance. Some indices perform better in bad years than others, and the same goes for with the good years. Compare and contrast your options to each other and to the historical S&P performance as well.

In addition to the various index options, IULs have a fixed account option as well. The fixed account offers just that; a fixed rate of return, regardless of stock market performance, for a one-year period.

This "fixed" strategy is great if you know that the stock market is going to tank. You can earn a fixed interest rate for that year, and then when the stock market rebounds, which it historically always does, then you can go back to an indexed strategy.

The Cap

There are two ways that the index works in an Indexed Universal Life policy:

1. You make the full amount of index's gains—called an "uncapped" strategy.

2. You earn up to something called a "cap."

With an uncapped index, you will receive all of the interest credited, based on the performance of the chosen index.

Some indexes have a cap on the interest credited, meaning that you will not earn higher than that rate, such as an 8% cap or a 12% cap. A cap is not necessarily a bad thing as interest credit overall can and has outperformed the stock market and, in some years, can even outperform the uncapped strategies.

Here's how a "cap" works:

Let's say the stock market returns an average of 12% in one year. The insurance company that holds your annuity has set its cap at 8%. The money in your annuity has earned 8% in interest.

Let's say the stock market returns an average of 3% in one year. The insurance company that holds your annuity has set its cap at 8%. How much interest did the money in your annuity earn? 3%.

Now let's say the market dropped 15% in one year. The insurance company that holds your annuity has set its cap at 8%. How much interest did the money in your annuity earn? 0%.

Your annuity didn't earn any interest that year, but more importantly, it didn't lose any interest either. Remember, interest equals money. If you had that money in the stock market, you would have lost the entire 15%.

Let's look at how a capped strategy compared to the stock market starting in 2000:

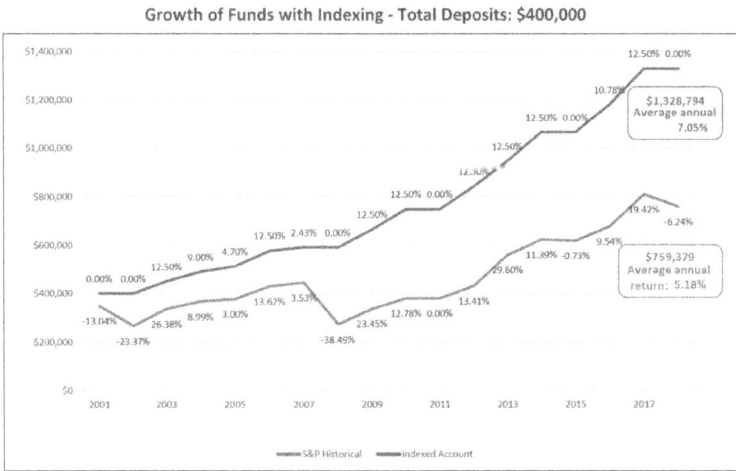

Growth of Funds with Indexing - Total Deposits: $400,000

Indexed Funds		S&P 500 2001 - 2018	
Beginning Value	$ 400,000	Beginning Value	$ 400,000
Final Value	$ 1,328,794	Final Value	$ 759,379
Largest Index Return	12.50%	Largest Index Return	29.60%
Lowest Index Return	0.00%	Lowest Index Return	-38.49%

Market returns assume S&P 500 Annual Returns Years 2001-2018, excluding dividends.

Indexed fund values do not include any costs.

Hypothetical example is for illustrative purposes only. This is not a prediction or guarantee of actual results, which will vary from those described.

D. Scott Kienk does not provide tax, legal or accounting advice, nor is it designed - nor intended - to be applicable to any person's individual circumstance. This material has been prepared for information purposes only, and is not intended to provide, and should not be relied on for, tax, legal or accounting advice. You should consult your own qualified tax, legal and accounting advisors before engaging in any transaction.

This chart is a historical illustration of $400,000 from 2000 to 2020 in the S&P compared to an indexed annuity with a 12.5% cap. In several years, the S&P paid higher than the capped strategy, and several years the cap strategy beat the S&P.[4]

But it's the overall performance that matters. Long term, even with a 12.5% cap, the indexed strategy beat out the stock market because of the loss prevention.

The decision on what index to choose, cap or uncapped, should be guided by its long-term performance. Work with your financial professional to compare what they did over a number of years and compare them in both the good and down years.

Crediting Over a Number of Years

Another concept to understand is crediting over a number of years. This means that your account is credited interest based on the number of years specified by the index.

Typically, indices offer a choice of a one-year or two-year crediting options. That time span is the look-back period that is used to determine the amount of interest that you will be credited, when you will be credited, and when you can change strategies.

With a one-year index, the amount of interest credited to your account will be based on the performance of the index over the last twelve months and you will be credited interest every year. You can change your strategy when it expires in one year.

With a two-year strategy, the amount of interest credited to your account will be based on the performance of the index over the last twenty-four months and you will be credited interest every two years. You can change your strategy when it expires in two years.

There are pros and a con to a two-year strategy.

I like the two-year strategy for two reasons:
- It spreads the volatility of the market over a two-year period rather than one
- The stock market typically performs better over a two-year period.

You are typically credited a higher amount on two-year strategies compared to one-year strategies, which will increase your overall rate of return.

However, I don't like the two-year strategy because your interest gets credited every two years instead of every year.

Here's my solution for that: Start the policy by putting 50% of your money in the one-year and 50% in the two year.

At the end of the one-year strategy, convert it to a two-year strategy. This way you will be getting alternating two-year crediting at the higher amount. In other words, you will get half of your two-year payment every year.

It will look like this:

1-Year	2-Year	2-Year	2-Year	2-Year	2-Year
2-Year	2-Year	2-Year	2-Year	2-Year	

Annual Reset

There is one more aspect of indexing that is often overlooked. It ties into the zero floor concept, and it has to do with something called the annual reset.

This simply means that whatever balance your IUL policy ended within any given year, that's the balance that you start with the next, and that balance is locked. Your balance will never drop due to stock market losses. Each year, when you are credited interest, your principle and interest *are* protected.

If your IUL policy is worth $100,000 after your interest is credited at the end of year one, then you start with $100,000 locked in for the next year.

If the stock market loses money in the second year, say 20%, then the starting balance on that *stock market account* is $80,000. But the balance in an IUL remains at $100,000.

There's a **big** difference between starting an account with $100,000 and starting with $80,000. The stock market account is having to make up for lost time—and time definitely equals money in this equation. It took upward of twenty-five years to recover losses from the stock market crash in 1929. It took close to five years to recover from the 2008 crash.

But here's the important question: why wait any length of time to recover when your money in the stock market when can be moving ahead immediately in a life-insurance index?

In an IUL, you don't have to make up for anything. You start at the same amount because you don't take losses.

Indexed Universal Life insurance is a great way to plan and create a no-stress retirement. Indexing is a huge part of that, and it is a strategy that is worth taking the time to learn about.

It is your money, your retirement, and you should know how your money is working for you every step of the way.

PART 3
Tax-Free Income

7 Tax-Free Income

Death, taxes, and dirty dishes. You can't escape them.

In the overview, I said, "The game (in retirement) is to make as much money as you can on the money that you have saved while you are working so that you have the income you need when you retire."

Income really is the most important part of the retirement equation. But "income" means "taxes." Right?

Not always.

There are just three ways to get income that is tax-free.

First: The Roth IRA. This is what people think when you say "tax-free retirement income."

The Roth IRA is, without doubt, a very powerful financial tool.

BUT, it has contribution rules and these rules limit how much money you can earn to even contribute as well as the amount of money that you can contribute, or if you earn too much, the rules prohibit you from contributing entirely.

Basically, it's punishing those who succeed in life and earn a good living. Not a good way to go.

Here's how the contribution levels work:[5]

Single Filers (MAGI)	Married Filing Jointly (MAGI)	Married Filing Separately (MAGI)	Maximum Contribution for individuals under age 50	Maximum Contribution for individuals age 50 and older
under $138,000	under $218,000	$0	$6,500	$7,500
$139,500	$219,000	$1,000	$5,850	$6,750
$141,000	$220,000	$2,000	$5,200	$6,000
$142,500	$221,000	$3,000	$4,550	$5,250
$144,000	$222,000	$4,000	$3,900	$4,500
$145,500	$223,000	$5,000	$3,250	$3,750
$147,000	$224,000	$6,000	$2,600	$3,000
$148,500	$225,000	$7,000	$1,950	$2,250
$150,000	$226,000	$8,000	$1,300	$1,500
$151,500	$227,000	$9,000	$650	$750
$153,000 & over	$228,000 & over	$10,000 & over	$0	$0

1. You may contribute simultaneously to a Traditional IRA and a Roth IRA (subject to eligibility) as long as the total contributed to all (Traditional and/or Roth) IRAs totals no more than $6,000 ($7,000 for those age 50 and over) for tax year 2022 and no more than $6,500 ($7,500 for those age 50 and over) for tax year 2023.

If you are single and earn $138k or less, or are married and earn $218K or less, your max ROTH contribution $6500 and $7500 if you are fifty years or older.

That's not a lot of money to save for retirement.

You can see the contribution limits decrease if you earn above $138k/$217k,

If you earn more than $153k single or $227k married, you cannot contribute at all. Many people I work with earn more than those limits.

Remember, this is the "succeed in life, earn a good income, and get punished" scenario.

The *second* way to get tax-free income is with tax-free municipal bonds. Bonds don't pay much anymore. And their risks are pretty high.

The *third* way uses the 7702 Section of the tax code. That is a cash value, life insurance contract. **Life insurance allows you to get income, tax-free.**

Think of an Indexed Universal Life policy as a giant Roth with no contribution limits and no income limits with a host of other benefits added in as well.

This is how it works.

How to get tax-free income from a cash value life insurance policy:

If you take a withdrawal from your account in a cash value life insurance policy, that income is taxable.

The proper way to get income from an IUL, the method that allows your income to be tax-free, is a loan.

When you take a loan from your policy, you are actually taking a loan against your future death benefit. Since payouts from the death benefits of life insurance are tax-free, loans are therefore tax-free as well.

Unlike the loans that you take from your bank, you do not need to pay interest on the loans while you are alive, and these loans do not have to be paid back in your lifetime—and the vast majority are not.

Instead, when you pass, the amount that you borrowed and the interest owed are deducted from taken out of your death benefit.

When loans are planned out in advance and shown on the insurance illustration, the death benefit amount already includes the reduction of the loan and interest costs.

These loans, combined with the **arbitrage** feature, described next, in Indexed Universal Life are the main reasons that IULs are a great financial tool.

A word of caution: While you can take a loan up to the full cash balance of your account, doing so could lapse your policy. If that happens, your loans are no longer loans against your death benefit, because the policy would no longer exist if it lapses. Therefore, your loans would be treated as withdrawals and are then subject to income tax. Not good.

If you need to cash out your account, you can prevent the policy from lapsing by greatly reducing the death benefit and paying the premium on the lowered benefit to keep the policy active, which in turn, keeps the loans tax-free. It's a great advantage of the flexibility of IULs.

The policy loan feature in an Indexed Universal Life cash-value life insurance policy makes this one of the most versatile, useful and best retirement vehicles you have available. Period.

8 Arbitrage

The first major secret sauce to the IUL is the zero floor. I like to call IUL's arbitrage feature its double secret sauce, because it's that good.

The second secret sauce to the IUL is the indexing that prevents stock market losses.

The third secret sauce....

I mentioned previously that when you borrow money from your IUL policy, you are taking a loan against your death benefit.

But, and this is another **_HUGE_** benefit, when you take a loan, you do not borrow from your cash value in the policy, you borrow from the insurance company. The death benefit is the collateral. The cash value in your account does not get reduced. Your cash value remains the same because you didn't borrow money from it.

You will notice that I capitalized, bolded, underlined, and italicized the word "huge" in the paragraph above, and here's why it is so important: since your cash balance is not reduced when you take a loan, you are credited interest on your entire account, every year, as if you never borrowed money from it. (Because, in fact, you didn't.)

If you have $200,000 cash value in your policy, and you borrow $50,000, you are still credited interest on your full $200,000, for the rest of your life, assuming the policy remains active.

Now, the loan is not free. You will owe interest to the insurance company. As previously stated, you will not have to pay loan back, nor the interest in your lifetime, because it will come out of the death benefit when you pass.

Here is why and how this is **SO VALUABLE** to you: in most years historically, the stock market has performed well and the amount of interest you are credited on the amount that you borrowed may be higher than the cost of the loan. In those cases, you are earning more than the cost of the loan.

The difference between the interest credited to you and the loan cost is called the ***arbitrage***.

If your annual interest credit is 10% and your loan cost is 5%, you will be credited 5% on the money that you borrowed.

Let that sink in.

You will have earned 5% interest on the money that you borrowed.

Read it again. If the index performs 5% above the interest charged on the loan, you will earn 5% interest on the money you borrowed.

AND, you will be credited with the arbitrage for rest of your life (as long as the policy remains in force). Or, until you pay it back, if you choose to pay it back.

Not a bad choice to make, at all.

Three times, I capitalized, bolded, underlined and italicized words, because those concepts are just that valuable.

Imagine going into your bank and telling the loan officer that you want a loan, and you want the bank to pay you interest on the money that you borrowed. That will never happen at a bank. However, that's exactly what happens with loans from Indexed Universal Life, daily, thousands and thousands of times.

There's got to be a catch, right?

Yes and no. If your credited interest is higher than your loan cost, you will be credited with the profit. But, if the market and your index do not perform well, your interest cost may be higher than your interest, so that year, the interest will be higher than your credit.

If your interest cost is 5% and your credit is only 3%, the loan cost you 2%, which happens to be a great rate. If the market crashes and your credit is zero, the loan would cost you the full 5% in that one year. It's still not a bad rate.

The good news is that the history of the market shows us that you may profit in many more years than not.

Historical Look Back at Arbitrage
Let's take a look at some arbitrage numbers.

In the last ten years the average arbitrage was 5.03%. That means that you were credited 5.03% on average on money that you borrowed. That's far better than paying interest, right?

In the last twenty 20 years, the average arbitrage was 2.67%,[6] and the in the last 30 years, the average arbitrage was 3.17%.

Using the lowest arbitrage average, to be conservative, if you earned an average of 2.67% on a $50,000 loan over 25 years, your profit would be $96,618.23.[7] You would have earned $96,000 interest on $50,000 that you borrowed. Yup, let that sink in.

And no, it is ***<u>NOT TOO GOOD TO BE TRUE</u>***. Capitalized, bolded, underlined and italicized, again.

Indexed Universal Life is the ONLY financial tool that offers all three of these benefits.

Using Arbitrage to Your Advantage
You may have heard about the concept that's called "Become Your Own Banker." This is an idea coined by an agent who loved the loan feature on a Whole Life contract.

Essentially, the idea of "Become your own Banker" is based on this idea of positive arbitrage. To recap: you take a loan. You pay say 5% in interest on the loan. But you're earning interest on the entire account balance. If that interest is more than the loan amount, then you're earning positive arbitrage.

If you make loan payments on this loan, then the money you're paying back to the policy is money you're paying yourself. This is a great use of this feature, and it works for anything—car loans, college loans, mortgage payments, even credit card payments. If it's done right, you could be making planned loan payments through your policy.

Positive arbitrage can even work with retirement income. **You can take loans out every year in retirement as tax-free income and still earn interest on your retirement income.**

Indexed Universal Life is the **ONLY** financial tool that can do this.

This incredible opportunity is there for you if you find an agent who knows how to unlock it. HINT. It is the **retirement specialist** that you seek.

PART 4
The Problem With the
"Usual" Retirement Strategies

9 The Fallacy of Pre-Tax Investing

Funds going into an Indexed Universal Life policy are after-tax monies, and so they can come out income-tax-free as policy loans.

That can equal a huge "yay!" especially in retirement.

However, some people are stunned when they learn that they have to pay tax upfront on the money they put in the policy. They believe they will lose the advantage of pre-tax investing.

Pre-tax investing became all the rage once pensions plans fell apart.

Pensions are going the way of the dodo bird (which is now extinct—the bird that is). There are few pension plans still in place, like with the Federal Government.

Pensions are great. You know exactly how much money you're going to get every month for the rest of your life.

But most of us work for companies that now use "defined contribution plans" like a 401(k) plan.

This means that the money you save for retirement goes into an account without being taxed up front.

This is "pre-tax investing."

The idea behind this is: you're making more money when you're working than when you retire, so if you put money away that isn't taxed up front, then you shouldn't pay as much tax when you retire.

This may come as a shock, because unless you actually run the numbers, you won't know if that's true.

To top it off, there is absolutely no financial advantage to pre-tax investing. None, nada, zilch.

Run the numbers if you don't believe me.

Not only that, pre-tax investing could cost you more in taxes. Yes, you read that right, pre-tax investing could cost you more.

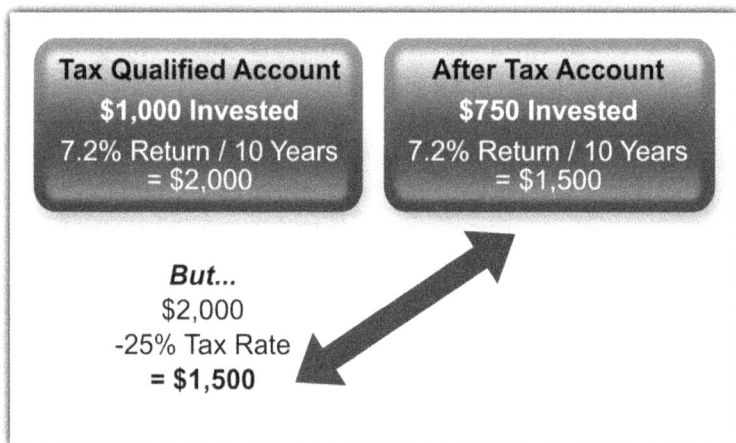

Tax Qualified Account
$1,000 Invested
7.2% Return / 10 Years
= $2,000

After Tax Account
$750 Invested
7.2% Return / 10 Years
= $1,500

But...
$2,000
-25% Tax Rate
= $1,500

Take a look at the chart above. If you invest $1,000 pretax and your money grows at 7.2% for 10 years, your account will double and you will have $2,000. Great. But assuming a 25% tax rate, you will have $1,500 after you pay the tax.

Looking that the same numbers with an after-tax account, after paying the same 25% tax on your initial $1,000, you have $750 left to invest. After the same 10 years earning the same 7.2%, you have $1,500. The exact same as the pre-taxed account.

There is absolutely no advantage to pre-tax investing. It's all smoke and mirrors.

So why the push for pre-tax investing? The answer can be found in who is pushing pre-tax investing:

> 1. Uncle Sam wants you to pay tax on the larger harvest at retirement than your smaller seed when you invest. You really didn't think the government was doing that for your benefit, did you?

> 2. Wall Street received increased fees because people feel obligated to invest in their pre-tax accounts in order to not miss out on their alleged "benefits," so they invest more and Wall Street lines their own pockets and celebrates. Plus, qualified plans are charged some of highest fees.

I also stated that pre-tax investing could cost you more. Think about this: Imagine if I came to you as a mortgage banker when you bought your home and I said, "*Listen, we have approved your mortgage loan application and we are going to lend you the money to buy your home. But, as for the interest rate, I'm NOT going to decide that today. What we're going to do is when your loan is due in thirty years. Whatever the interest rate is at that year, I'm going to apply it to your mortgage, from the first day you took out the loan.*"

Would you ever take that loan with an unknown interest rate?

Most of you would say absolutely not. You have no idea what the interest rates are going to be in thirty years, and you don't want to take that gamble. **But that's *exactly* what you are doing with these Traditional IRAs and 401(k)s.**

We said, "*I don't care what the tax rates are going to be in the future, I just want these tax deductions now*," and the government knew that.

Think about all the stimulus money going out, the flailing economy, near-record inflation, incredibly high national debt, the out-of-control government spending. Which direction do **you** think taxes are going? Think they may be higher in 15 or 20 years in the future when you will have to pay taxes on all your income from your pre-tax plans?

We have no idea where for sure taxes are going to be in 10, 20, 30 years. Most likely, we are probably at the lowest tax brackets we will ever see in our lifetimes. Do you want to bet that taxes will be lower when you retire?

Now that you know the truth, you won't be fooled by pre-tax investing.

Indexed Universal life allows you to pay taxes on your seed— the money you're putting into your account upfront, when you know exactly how much tax you are going to have to pay and before they rise.

You never have to bet on taxes going up or down when your money is in an IUL.

10 Why Not Invest in the Stock Market

I have killed one "sacred cow" about retirement planning. Pre-tax investing doesn't give you any advantage.

Here's the other one: the stock market.

"Everyone," or so we're told, puts their retirement funds in the stock market.

Unfortunately, the stock market is not the panacea of profits and earnings that we would like it to be.

Sure, the market has a long-term history of increases, but it's not a steady climb. There are a lot of crashes along the way. These ups and down—the volatility—can be deadly to your account, especially if you are nearing or in the withdrawal phase of retirement.

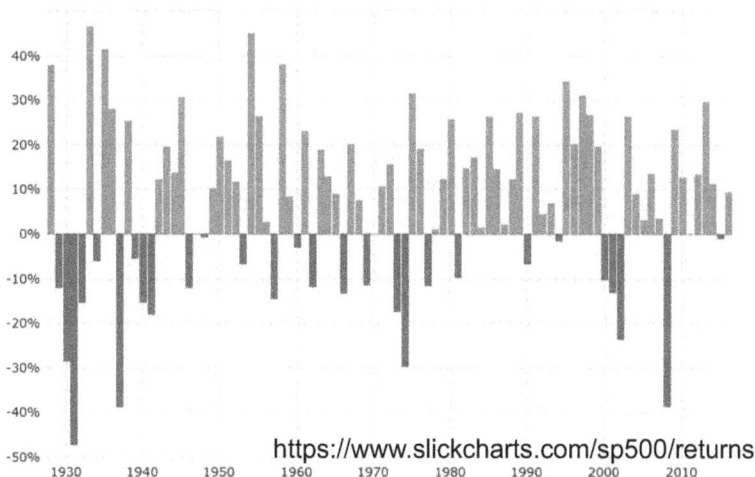

https://www.slickcharts.com/sp500/returns

The final days of 2021 ended one of the biggest and longest bull runs in stock market history. The powers that be kept the market in this upward swing artificially for many years. That isn't "business as usual." The average time between a market high and a market crash is around eight to eleven years. Many investors have forgotten about all the crashes shown in the chart above.

The Fallacy of Averages
Wall Street likes to talk about average returns: 2020 averaged 28.71% and 2009 averaged 26.69%. They brag and they brag.

Would you be surprised if I told you that average performance means nothing?

I say that because the volatility between those "average dates" can destroy your account.

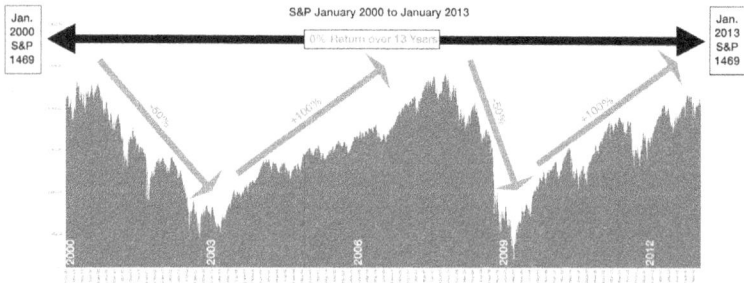

*finance.yahoo.com

Using rounded numbers, From Jan. 2000 to Jan. 2013, the market dropped 50%, then rose 100%, then dropped 50% and rose 50%. It started at 1,469 and ended at 1,469.

Thirteen years and you didn't gain a penny. Thirteen long years and you ended up where you started.

The performance totaled approximately 100% (-50% +100%,

-50% +100%) across the timespan. Dividing the total 100% performance by its 13-year duration shows that the market performed an approximate average of 7.69% from during that period.

However, the market's volatility—its ups and downs—over those 13 years, destroyed all investor gains. The S&P in January 2000 was the same as January 2013, 13 years later.

Investors got a near zero return over those 13 years, even though the average performance was 7.69%. That's the menace of stock market volatility.

Taking money out during down years means that you are cannibalizing your principle, which can be a recipe for financial disaster.

It's those crashes that hurt, the volatility. If you lose 50%, you need 100% just to break even.

Wall Street doesn't like to talk about volatility, but boy do they love to shout "averages" from the rooftops!

That said, most investors are shocked to learn that the lifetime average of the stock market is just over 5%. Sure, there are lots of double-digit return years, but add in the volatility and the market doesn't sound as rosy.

Volatility is especially brutal when you are in the withdrawal phase of retirement.

One of the most common withdrawal theories is the 4% rule. Take out 4% of your retirement balance annually, and the market returns—which average over 5% long-term—will keep your account balance healthy.

Great theory, but the stock market does not agree.

Year	Beg. Cash	S&P 500	Withdrawal	End Cash
1/2000	$1,000,000	-9.10%	$40,000	$881,306
1/2001	$861,306	-11.89%	$40,000	$712,918
1/2002	$712,918	-22.10%	$40,000	$510,267
1/2003	$510,267	28.68%	$40,000	$598,827
1/2004	$598,627	10.88%	$40,000	$609,722
1/2005	$609,722	4.91%	$40,000	$586,785
1/2006	$586,785	15.79%	$40,000	$623,763
1/2007	$623,763	5.49%	$40,000	$606,173
1/2008	$606,173	-37.13%	$40,000	$342,282
1/2009	$342,282	26.46%	$40,000	$374,757
1/2010	$374,757	15.06%	$40,000	$378,070
1/2011	$378,070	2.11%	$40,000	$338,591
1/2012	$338,591	16.05%	$40,000	$342,787
1/2013	$342,787	32.39%	$40,000	$399,358
1/2014	$399,358	13.69%	$40,000	$402,387
1/2015	$402,387	1.38%	$40,000	$359,614
1/2016	$359,614	14.06%	$40,000	$351,343
1/2017	$351,343	21.83%	$40,000	$376,070
1/2018	$376,070	-4.38%	$40,000	$315,944
1/2019	$315,944	31.19%	$40,000	$345,652

The chart above shows a retiree starting with $1 million in 2000 and taking out 4% of the starting account balance annually, which is $40,000, for twenty years.

The average performance of the stock market historically was 7.87% over those twenty years. But with just a 4% withdrawal, the account balance at the end of the twenty years was dropped way down to just $345,652.

With this scenario, it's just a few short years to bankruptcy and/or a retirement job as a Walmart greeter.

How can you earn an average of 7.87%, take out just 4% annually, and have your account drop from $1 million to just $345,000? Volatility. Remember, that 7.87% average is not annual returns, it's just a long-term average.

Volatility kills income. Income is what makes or breaks a good retirement.

I mentioned above that Wall Street doesn't like to talk about volatility. They also don't like to talk income and withdrawals in retirement because that's where the stock market concept falls apart.

The stock market is a great place to grow your money in your working years. You can afford the volatility; you can even afford market crashes. Why? Because you have a paycheck. You don't need that money for many years. Time is one your side. Not so when nearing retirement and in retirement. The time that it takes to recover from market crashes is time that you cannot afford.

But once you transition from work to retirement, your financial needs change. Instead of contributing you are now withdrawing. Your financial strategy needs to change as well.

You need to eliminate volatility. This is why the zero floor and annual reset features in an Indexed Universal Life policy are so valuable in retirement

CHAPTER 11 Why You Have Not Heard of IULs

You might be saying to yourself, "If Indexed Universal Life is such a great financial tool, why has my advisor not told me about them?" Good question.

Your financial advisor is a fiduciary, which means that he/she has a legal requirement to do what is in the best interest of their clients. They do just that, but they are limited to the resources that they can offer.

How so? Most financial advisors are licensed to sell securities. This means they can play the stock market with your money. Wall Street types typically don't have the proper licenses to sell IULs, so not only can they not offer them to you, they often don't understand how they work and their benefits.

So, why don't they get the licenses? Another good question. Their skyscraper institutions won't let them.

Why? In a word, greed.
    1. They don't want you to know how IULs may outperform the stock market.

    2. Wall Street can earn far more in fees keeping you in the stock market than by selling an IUL.

Fee-Based
First, it's important to define "financial advisor." This is an

often overly-used term, but it is most commonly attached to something called a "registered advisor." This means the financial advisor has the correct license to advise you on what investments—primarily stock market—he thinks are good for you. We are using "financial advisor" for both here.

Financial advisors are licensed to manage your money in the stock market and charge a fee. They make money from your money regardless of whether you see them on your statements or not.

There are strict rules that govern them, and they are bound, by law, to be your "fiduciary."

A fiduciary is someone who is supposed to have your best interests at heart when it comes to money. That means that they are not supposed to sell you financial products that benefit them more than others in fees or commissions rather than it being the best choice for you. Most financial advisors that you're going to run into are going to be a fiduciary by law.

Financial advisors who work with stock market investments get paid with a fee. And they get paid that fee as long as you keep your money with them in the stock market. If you have your money in the stock market for thirty years, then your advisor is going to make thirty-years' worth of fees.

I'm sure you're familiar with the old adage, "Always work with a financial advisor who charges a fee, rather than commissions."

Supposedly, somehow fees are far better than commissions. We'll let you be the judge of that once you know some of the fine print of both.

Financial advisors charge a fee to:
1. Give you a financial plan.
2. Keep your money in the stock market.

Financial advisors that I know charge anywhere from $5,000 to $12,000 to give you a financial plan for your money. Their advice is based on two things:
1. the amount of money you have to invest, and
2. the amount of risk you want to take with it.

Risk here is defined as how much money you're willing to lose when the stock market goes south.

They also may show you how your money is going to produce income when you retire, but many financial advisors don't go there. They can't guarantee you that income. They can show you hypotheticals based on past performance of the stock market, but make no mistake: they cannot guarantee you any of that.

If you want to spend thousands of dollars for that service, that's fine.

Here's the real issue that you need to know about.

Financial advisors also charge you a fee to manage your money in the stock market.

According to Nerd Wallet, that fee ranges from .25% to 1%.[8] I don't know where they're getting their information because I know some advisors who charge 1.5%, some even 2.0%.

Whatever the case, those fees are taken directly from your balance and may never even show up on your statements.

If that financial advisor is making 1% on your money, know this. They are going to make 1% no matter if you lose money or make money in the market. Let me rephrase that: they are making a fee even when you are losing money in the stock market.

You may know all this and say, "Well, Scott, I want to make sure my financial advisor is incentivized to make me money."

That's great when the stock market is doing well. But what happens when everyone loses money in the stock market because the market crashed? No financial advisor is going to be able to make money when everyone else is losing money in the stock market.

I read a story in the online magazine Market Watch about a woman who had a million dollars.[9] She's a single mom and wanted to use that money for her daughter's college and what was left was going to her retirement.

Her advisor took his 1.5% fees, which was $15,000 the first year. In 2021, she lost money in the stock market, which brought her account balance down to $800,000, and her advisor took his 1.5% yearly fee, which was another $12,000. So now, the woman's account was down to $788,000.

"I'm not sure what my financial advisor is doing for me. I don't know what he's supposed to be doing," the woman lamented.

Sadly, the advice the columnist gave her was to find a financial advisor who only charged one percent in fees.

She wouldn't be losing as much money—I guess that was their reasoning.

Financial advisors have a lot on their plate. But when is the last time your advisor called you and said, "We need to talk about putting your money in cash because that's where it's going to be safest right now."

Or

"We need to sit down and talk about your income plan, make sure it's still on track."

Most people don't hear from their advisor when the market starts falling. Did your advisor call you in the beginning of 2022 and say, "The market is dropping, we need to make some changes."?

In the spring of that same year, when the market had dropped for three straight months, did you get a call then?

What about June, after six months of losses, did your advisor call then?

Fall? December? The overwhelming response when I talk to people is, "*No, my advisor never called.*"

Like the single mom above, the advisor may meet with you from time to time—but nothing changes. And there is no safe money at all involved. How could it? It's the stock market.

Wall Street Commissions
Fee-based advisors dominate your choices for portfolio management. The reason, always, is because they are your "fiduciary." They are supposed to have your best financial interests at heart.

The prevailing idea is that commission guys—they're out to

get your money.

These are the salespeople who make sure that they're getting the most out of their sale of financial products to you.

How true is that?

Sometimes, it's exactly what happens. Brokers make a commission every time they sell a stock in your portfolio or buy a new one.

These are the men—and occasionally a woman—who used to be portrayed in movies vying for attention on the floor of the New York stock exchange. Now most of those deals are done by computer—it's faster. More convenient.

Whatever the case, these stock brokers are making money every time they buy and sell stock in your portfolio. And that commission comes straight out of your portfolio balance.

Sometimes, unethical stockbrokers will "churn" accounts, meaning they will buy and sell stock far more than is necessary. Why? They make a commission every time they buy and sell stock in your portfolio.

The stock market has its uses, but it is not for the faint of heart. You have to have a strong stomach because you're going to watch your money go up and down—and your emotions are going to follow.

It's kind of like a roller coaster.

You're elated at the top. It's sickening as you fly downward to the bottom. When you're at the bottom, if you still have the contents of your stomach intact, you're glad to get out of the car and on to solid ground.

When I sell an IUL to a client, they get stock market protection, tax-free income, earn the arbitrage on their loans, and receive a host of other valuable benefits.

What do I get? A commission, but commissions are paid by the insurance companies, not by clients, so it never costs them a penny out of their account like the fees from advisors.

All of my client's money goes into their IUL, and that's what earns interest. And that gives me something far greater than a commission. It gave me peace of mind knowing that my client wasn't going to lose money, and I wasn't taking any money out of their policy.

When you buy an IUL, either Wall Street doesn't get the money, or it gets taken out of the stock market. Wall Street hates having money taken from them.

When you purchase an IUL, it means that you're spending money that your Wall-Street-incentivized "fiduciary" would otherwise be making money on, year after year after year.

Are you funding *your* retirement or *their* wallet?

PART 5
The Ins and Outs of IULs

12 IUL Illustrations and AG49

Now that we've talked about why IULs give you want you really want in retirement, it's time to educate you on how you know you're getting all that I've told you about.

The insurance industry is all about making sure you know exactly what you're getting. They do this with an insurance policy "illustration" which is designed to show future performance based on historical performance.

It's a proposal, the precursor to the contract. It's what the insurance company gives you to show what the insurance contract may do.

Illustrations are important. They are also highly regulated. The government wants to make sure the insurance companies aren't cheating you. That's fair.

Known as AG 49, the regulations "were adopted by the National Association of Insurance Commissioners in 2015 to rein in IUL illustrations that were showing consumers unrealistic returns." Sounds reasonable and a good thing for consumers.

But unfortunately, the regulations limit the ability of IUL illustrations to show you their true historical performance. Insurance companies are forced to project lower returns than what is historically accurate.

It is important to note that AG49 does not affect the performance of the policy in any way, only the presale illustration is restricted.

Since annuity illustrations, which are also issued by insurance companies, are not restricted in this manner. It has been speculated that the real reason it was done was that Uncle Sam does not like tax-free investing and wanted to downplay their performance. Who knows for sure?

Here's a partial index performance table from a recent client illustration:

Indexed Interest Strategy	Maximum Permitted Illustrated Rate*	30 Year Historical Average**
1-Yr Capped S&P 500	5.88%	6.32%
2-Yr S&P 500	6.05%	7.82%
1-Yr J.P. Morgan Mozaic II	6.05%	8.05%
2-Yr J.P. Morgan Mozaic II	6.05%	10.55%
1-Yr NYSE Zebra Edge	6.05%	7.86%
2-Yr NYSE Zebra Edge	6.05%	9.30%
1-Yr Choice Plus J.P. Morgan Mozaic II	7.12%	10.35%
1-Yr Choice Plus NYSE Zebra Edge	7.12%	9.67%

The right column shows the historical average and the middle column from the right shows "Maximum Permitted Illustrated Rate" as permitted by AG49. As you can see, the difference between several of them is tremendous.

Fortunately, insurance companies are able to state the actual historical average, they just can't base their illustrated projections on them.

AG49 also limited the arbitrage percentage that insurance companies are allowed to use to 1%, and AG49-A, effective Dec. 2020, reduced it even further, to 0.5%. Arbitrage, as you learned in a previous section, is very important to how you make money on your money and keep your income steady.

What that all means to you is that you may see higher performance that what is illustrated.

I included this information in this book, because when agents explain to clients that the historical performance is actually higher than the illustrated rate, they often think that the agent is trying to pull a fast one, maybe exaggerating the benefits. This doubt reduces the agent's credibility unfairly.

They are not deceiving you; historical returns *are* typically higher than shown in IUL illustrations and AG49 is the reason.

13 The Underwriting Process

While Indexed Universal Life is designed as a financial tool, it is life insurance. And as such, you need to qualify medically to be able to purchase it.

This is an important step of the process. Not everyone qualifies for life insurance. Even if you don't medically qualify, there are still ways for you to take advantage of Indexed Universal Life benefits even if the policy is not taken out on you.

You can expect that your medical history is scrutinized when you apply for an Indexed Universal Life insurance contract. This history is kept confidential to the insurance company. Without it, you cannot get the contract. The underwriters need to know if you are a good risk for the death benefit they are giving you.

Here's how it works: In the application process, you will be asked to provide the name of your doctors, a list of your past and present medications, any medical conditions you have and surgeries that you have had among other things. The insurance company will also check your medical history through the Medical Information Bank.

Other factors you will need to include on the application are gender, height/weight, family history, occupation, and hobbies. They will also look at your driving record and credit score to help determine if you are a good risk. Tobacco and drug use are big factors as well. If you smoke or chew tobacco, you may still receive the insurance, but at a higher rate, which means that the insurance (the death benefit) is going to cost you more and you're not going to receive as much.

Sometimes the insurance company will send a medical technician to you to obtain your weight and a blood sample. In cases where medical records clearly show that you are very healthy, they may choose not to send the technician.

NOTE: Lying on the application is a sure way to get denied. I had a client who was denied because he didn't disclose his tobacco use, and it showed up in his medical records. Had he disclosed it, he would have been accepted.

Both your acceptance and the cost of the policy will be based on these conditions:
- If you are in very good health, you may be classified as "preferred" which is the lowest cost bracket.

- You may be classified as "standard" if you have some minor issues.

- If you have certain medical conditions, the policy may be "rated" which means your cost will be higher.

Don't let medical conditions prevent you from applying. Unless there is a life-threatening illness, most applications will be approved as long as the medical condition(s) is under control.

When quoting your policy, your agent should ask some basic medical history and quote you in the appropriate classification, but the exact classification and cost won't be known until the insurance company completes its underwriting process. So, don't be surprised if the actual cost is different than what your agent quoted.

If you do not qualify medically for the policy, you do have options. This is what I mentioned in the introduction.

You do not need to be the named "insured" on the policy. Even if you are using the policy for your financial needs, the insured can be anyone that you have "insurable interest" in, such as a spouse or a child. They would be the insured, but you would own the policy and take advantage of the financial benefits.

For business owners, you can use a key employee in addition to your spouse or child as the insured since you have "insurable interest" in that employee.

Again, this is something that your insurance agent will help you with, and this is why you need an agent who understands how this process works. Not all agents do.

14 How Safe is Indexed Universal Life?

So far I have covered the great benefits of Indexed Universal Life. But now you may be asking, how safe are they? How safe are the insurance companies that issue them?

Let's start the conversation with what most think is the bedrock of safety: banks. Most people have tremendous regard for the safety of banks, but they are not as safe as most believe.

Let's cut to the chase. Insurance companies are very safe; banks, not so much. Here's the why and how:

Any financial advisor who has your best interests at heart is going to tell you that you need to have an emergency savings account. In other words, that you build and maintain a reserve.

Life happens. Cars break down or your kid gets in a fender bender. Your hot water heater fails right when you need to have shoulder surgery. It is vital to have a reserve specifically set aside for life's unforeseen events.

Banks have emergencies that they need reserves for as well. They need many millions, or if the bank is large enough, then billions of dollars, to handle emergencies as they arise.

Insurance companies also run into emergencies, and they too need reserves.

That reserve amount is what determines the safety of the financial institution and the laws governing reserve accounts for banks and for insurance companies differ greatly.

Banks Use Fractional Reserves
In the banking industry, the law allows banks to engage in "fractional-reserve banking." That means that banks are required to hold only a portion of deposits in liquid assets. The rest is able to be loaned to borrowers.

Let's say you make a $100 deposit. That money isn't "in the bank," as most people believe. Just a small portion of it is kept on the bank's balance sheet and the rest of that deposit is lent out.

How much is a bank legally required to keep? Ten percent. They are required to keep just ten percent of their deposits. Out of that $100 deposit that you "put in the bank," the bank only keeps $10. The $90 remaining is loaned out.

Why does your local bank lend out so much money? It makes a lot of money on the compounding interest it charges on all the money it lends.

The money a bank keeps in reserves is for one very important purpose: to prevent the panic that can arise if customers make a "run" on the bank. This is what happened when the stock market crashed in 1929. Word got out that banks didn't have enough cash on hand to meet all the immediate withdrawal demands, and depositors "ran" to the bank to withdraw their cash and crashed the banks.

By the way, from 2008 to 2012, 465 banks failed while only three insurance providers failed. [10]

Bank "runs" and failures happen. It's not something that happened just "back then." When the news broke that Silicon Valley Bank (one of the largest banks in the US at the time) was going to fail in early 2023, people who had their money in that banking institution started withdrawing their money.

Silicon Valley Bank, which was already teetering on the brink of collapse, got pushed over the edge because it did not have enough money to meet all the immediate withdrawal demands. The FDIC took control of the bank. There were more complicated factors involved in its failure, but it all stemmed from them not having enough in reserves to cover what they needed.

FDIC Insurance
Everyone knows that all banks are insured by the federal government up to $250,000 by the FDIC, the Federal Deposit Insurance Corporation.

When people get antsy about banks, like they did in early 2023, people start worrying about whether or not their money is safe in their local banks.

The FDIC's Reserves
When a bank fails, we believe that the FDIC is going to pay each depositor in that bank up to $250,000. But that's not what really happens. The FDIC sometimes pays depositors, but that is rare. What usually happens when a bank fails? The FDIC finds another bank to take on the failing bank's liabilities. That means that you may not see your money for months until the FDIC finds another bank to take over and make good on your deposits. Only if the FDIC is unable to find a suitable bank to take over the failed banks will it indemnify depositors directly (meaning it will pay out money directly), up to the limit.

The FDIC itself has reserves as well, currently at $124.5 billion and a $100 billion line of credit from the US Treasury (2023), but that only covers 1.26% of ALL bank deposits.[11]

According to Barron's, the FDIC reported that at the end of 2022, its reserves were less than half of the $262 billion that would be needed if there was a catastrophic bank failure and everyone in the US wanted to withdraw their funds up to that $250,000.[12]

Your money is not safe if you can't withdraw it when you need it. Banks are not as "safe" as many people envision.

Insurance Company Reserves: One to One
Insurance companies are just the opposite of banks when it comes to reserves.

They are required to have 100 percent of their annual liabilities in reserve. They usually have much more so that they can cover any contingent claims that arise.

That means that insurance companies have enough cash on hand to pay 100 percent of the claims of all of their customers in any given year. That's 100 percent, compared to just ten percent for banks.

Most insurance companies have a stellar financial reputation. In the world of money, "stellar" means that they have a lot of money in reserves and those funds are invested very conservatively. You can see what an insurance company's reputation is by the rating it is given. If it's A or above (or the equivalent of A or above), then you know that the company has the kind of reserves you want in an insurance company, and that company knows how to invest those funds so that the funds are always there to pay out all their obligations to those they insure. That includes IUL pay outs.

Insurance History 101
This is a quick history lesson to help you understand why insurance companies are safer than banks.

The purpose of insurance companies is to transfer and absorb risk. When you buy insurance, the risk is transferred from you to the insurance company.

It's always better if you have a cushion when you fall. The "fall" is the risk. The "cushion" is what the insurance company provides.

Insurance companies were formed in the early 1600s as a way for ship owners to mitigate the risk they were taking by ferrying very valuable cargo across the ocean. The ship owners wanted to find a way to "cushion" any "fall" they may experience with cargo being carted off by pirates, or sunk by a nasty storm, or whatever disasters could happen to the ship and cargo in transit.

First, the ship owner would divide the cargo up and have it carried on multiple ships. That way, if one ship lost its cargo, then not all would be lost.

But there was another layer of protection that these ship owners were seeking. Before a fleet of ships set sail, the merchants and ship owners would go to a coffee shop in London owned by a man named Edward Lloyd. (You may be familiar with "Lloyds of London," the premier company that handles specialty insurance; it was started by that man, hence the name.)

These merchants and ship owners would meet up with investors at Lloyd's Coffee House. These investors would take on the risk of the voyage for a set "premium" or payment. They would sign their names at the bottom of the ship's manifest (hence the term "underwriting"), indicating what share of the cargo they were taking responsibility for. There were always a number of these "underwriters" because no one investor wanted to take responsibility for all the cargo any one ship was carrying.

Fast forward a couple of hundred years to the middle 1800s. An American named Elizur Wright became America's first state insurance regulator in Massachusetts. His family helped fugitive slaves. He went to school with John Brown and ran an abolitionist newspaper. In other words, he had a strong sense of what was right and good. He was also appalled that old men would auction off the death benefits of their life insurance policies to fund their old age. He fought—and won—for insurance reform. The main issue was requiring insurance companies to pay surrender values, and to do this, they figured out how to calculate an insurance company's reserves. The standards were very strict, and they still hold to this day. This reserve system that Wright created turned the insurance industry into some of the safest financial institutions on earth.

Insurance companies are good at handling the "fall"—the risk that they take on when they insure someone. They do that by having a very deep cushion. Their reserves are possibly the best. This is why when there is a flood or fire or other natural disaster, the insurance companies are the institutions that pay claims and help people rebuild their lives.

Insurance Reserves
It's the reserves that insurance companies carry that make them save. But how are these reserves managed?

To recap: Banks follow a fractional reserve system as I defined above. Insurance companies do not.

Permanent life insurance companies, the companies that issue IULs, are required by federal and state law to have annual dollar-for-dollar reserves as I noted above. Unlike banks who just keep a ten percent reserve, insurance companies are required to have 100 percent of their annual liabilities in reserve.

How are those reserves managed?

The General Fund
An insurance company works out of something called a "general fund."

Premiums that are paid to the insurance company go into that fund. Your IUL premiums go into that fund.

It is an account that's highly regulated by federal and state laws. The rules under which an insurance company can manage that general fund are very strict. This is the first layer of protection.

The insurance company is considered a "fiduciary." They are entrusted to handle your money for your future benefit, not for their own profit. Thus, it must submit a substantial annual report to all the states it is licensed to operate in, and it must submit its general fund to be audited every year.

If you ever read the fine print of a life insurance contract, it says that your payments are subject to the "claims paying ability" of the insurance carrier. This simply means that an insurance carrier is able to pay its claims or losses in a timely manner.

How can they do this? Because they have those reserves—in abundance.

Many of the best insurance carriers have reserves in excess of 100 percent of their claims paying ability. That's the hallmark of a top institution. This is the second layer of protection.

State Guaranty Associations
Every state has a State Guaranty Association which acts as a third layer of protection. The exact name may vary, but their functions are identical. They regulate and protect the industry at the state level. These state guaranty associations will pay claimants in the unlikely event that an insurance company becomes insolvent and cannot pay. Coverage is limited and varies by state. This offers a third layer of protection.

Reinsurance
The fourth layer of protection reinsurance. Insurance companies buy insurance on themselves to make sure they can handle all the claims made in case of major claims events.

Recap
The *first layer* of cushion that your money has in an insurance contract is the way the General Fund is managed—conservatively.

The *second layer* comes from the reserves every insurance company is required to maintain. This is the dollar-for-dollar system noted above. It's called the "Legal Reserve System."

This *third layer* is the State Guaranty Fund.

The *fourth layer* of protection—reinsurance—insures against an insurance company's inability to pay claims.

These four layers form the bottom line; insurance companies are safe, very safe.

Who?

Here's something else to consider: regardless of the product or service, consumers prefer to buy from companies they know. It's only natural. There are over 5,900 insurance companies in the US, but people only know a handful. Why? Advertising. Advertising, paid for by clients.

IULs are insurance contracts, so you want to make sure that the policy you are purchasing comes from a highly rated insurance company, one that has a surplus of reserves. You want an insurance company that has an "A" rating or equivalent.

Don't be afraid of buying from an insurance company that you do not know. Rather than their name, judge them by the strength of their reserves, financial ratings, and the value of their policy offering. You just might find them better than the companies who spend tens of millions of dollars a year on advertising and skyscrapers.

The assurance and safety of an Indexed Universal Life contract comes from an insurance company that has a good rating, and that rating is based on their reserves and how they manage that money. This is what keeps your money safe.

15 IUL Costs

Even though Indexed Universal Life is designed as a financial tool, it is life insurance after all, and as such, the life insurance component of the plan does have a cost.

The IRS code requires that there is a certain amount of death benefit, and that amount is related to the level of cash in the plan. The higher the amount that you contribute to the saving component, the higher the death benefit needs to be.

Because IULs are very flexible, the death benefit can change as needed. In a properly constructed plan wealth-building plan, the death benefit varies and will match the minimum needed as the cash value changes. This allows the cost of the insurance component to be as low as possible.

Rather than a typical round-number death benefit such as $300,000, you may see $286,358. The odd number is the exact minimum of death benefit needed in relation to the cash to keep the policy in "life insurance" status. The lower the death benefit, the lower the cost.

Keep in mind that the cost of the insurance component varies as it is based on the age and health of the client. The earlier that you start the policy, the lower the cost.

Overall, the lifetime cost of the insurance, divided by the

number of years in the plan, is very competitive with other financial options.

IRA, mutual fund and 401(k) costs

Don't forget that you no matter where you invest, you will have costs. The average costs for mutual funds in your IRAs, 401(k)s, and brokerage can be quite high. A Forbes article states: "According to a study published in the Financial Analyst Journal that was authored by finance professors at the University of California Davis, University of Virginia, and Virginia Tech, the average expense ratio is 1.19%. And, "the average hidden cost of mutual funds is 1.44%." [13]

While that annual 1% fee may not sound like a lot, multiply it by 20 or 30 over the life of your plan and see what you get.

Demos.org, the online site of a US think tank, states that 401(k) "...fees can be substantial: over a lifetime, fees can cost a median-income two-earner family nearly $155,000 and consume nearly one-third of their investment returns."[14] Wow!

Brokerage Costs

Costs are high in brokerage accounts as well, especially if you are working with an advisor.

According to Nerd Wallet, that fee ranges from .25% to 1%.[15] I don't know where they're getting their information because I know some advisors who charge 1.5%, some even 2.0%.

Whatever the case, those fees are taken directly from your balance and may never even show up on your statements.

If that financial advisor is making 1% on your money, know this. They are going to make 1% no matter if you lose money or make money in the market. Let me rephrase: they are making a fee even when you are losing money in the stock market.

One Caveat

While IUL fees are competitive over the lifetime of the plan, it is important to understand that they are front-loaded, most of the fees happen in the first ten years of the plan. The fee goes down from there, and reduces rapidly.

This is relevant to you in two ways:

1. The cash value is low in the first few years. Therefore, you need to let the policy grow for at least five to seven years, maybe longer, before taking loans. If you can't wait that long, IULs may not be the best option for you.

2. Over the life of the policy, IULs offer very competitive costs, but since most of the expenses happen in the first ten years, it will be too expensive if you only want to keep the policy for just a short time. If you keep the policy for its intended purpose of a lifetime of benefits, overall costs will be very competitive because the longer you keep the policy, the lower its cost.

All financial products have a cost. It's important to know how much and for how long that cost is going to be incurred, and if that cost is paid directly by you or by the financial or insurance institution that is handling your money. It is your money, after all.

PART 6
The Good Stuff

.

16 IUL: The Great Financial Tool

The ability of Indexed Universal Life to offer competitive returns, no stock market losses, tax-free income, and earn interest on loans (the arbitrage) makes it a very powerful and versatile financial tool.

The death benefit can be your legacy for the next generation. That's the insurance portion of the contract. That can be the defining feature for some, and if it is, tell your agent so the policy can be built to maximize the death benefit.

If you're talking retirement income, and you need decent accumulation and protection, then IULs can be customized to maximize those benefits.

Whether your goal is accumulation, retirement income, risk mitigation, tax reduction, or helping the next generation, IULs are a great option because they are powerful, multipurpose, and very flexible. They can be customized for your needs and adjusted as your goals change.

Let's take a look at some ways the cash value portion of the Indexed Universal Life insurance policy can work for you. It's done through the intentional use of the policy loan feature, and once you understand that, your world can open up.

Following are seven of the most often uses of IULs as a financial tool.

Financial Tool #1: Tax-Free Retirement Income

This is a book about no-stress retirement. An Indexed Universal Life policy gives you that. In spades.

This chapter will be short and sweet to prevent it from looking like it was written by the Department of Redundancy Department.

Here is the key: setting up the IUL policy correctly and accessing the policy loans in the right way.

This gives you income, potentially for the rest of your life, and you don't have to pay income tax on it. IULs are a giant ROTH without all the strings attached.

Unlike a Roth, IULs have:
- No income restriction
- No annual contribution limits
- No withdrawal limitations

Does it get any better?

- Here's a list of the additional benefits:
- Tax-free income with policy loans
- Take income anytime
- Stock market protection
- Competitive earnings
- Earning arbitrage interest on money borrowed
- No penalties, ever
- Living benefits
- Tax-free inheritance

Need I say more?

Financial Tool #2—College Funding
(with Retirement Income!)

I'm using college funding as a way to showcase what an IUL can do. However, this concept works for any large purchase, any time you need money.

Indexed Universal Life is a perfect financial tool for college planning for a number of reasons:
- College is a large expense.
- You know far in advance that the bill is coming.
- You know when you will need the money.
- You can project with relative accuracy how much you may need.
- The money that you spend on college will be returned to you as interest from the IUL, throughout the rest of your life.
- You will get a host of other benefits from the policy using money that would otherwise have to come out of your pocket and never be seen again.

It's a match made in financial heaven.

After student loans, scholarships and grants, the balance of the college costs can be paid by you writing a check to the college or using parent loans, both of which costs you money.

Instead of paying that balance yourself out of your pocket, you can run the money through an IUL and pay the balance with a loan from the policy. With the IUL you will get paid interest on the money that you borrowed for the college expenses using the arbitrage concept that I covered in Chapter 8, *Arbitrage*.

Would you rather *pay* interest on a parent loan or *get paid* interest?

Working with a college planning expert, the process starts by estimating the cost of the school.
Then subtract anticipated grants based on financial need as well as the average amount of scholarships and student loans you expect your children to receive.

The balance will need to be paid out-of-pocket, by parent loans or preferably by loans from an Indexed Universal Life Insurance policy.

An IUL policy is best utilized by allowing your premiums to grow and then paying the school bills with loans. Once college is paid for, allow your account balance to grow to provide lifetime income in retirement. With that strategy in mind, a budget is set for the premium with both short- and long-term expectations.

When working with a family, I utilize as much expiring debt as possible, so the extra money needed for funding is as low as possible. What I mean by that, is that I look for money the family is currently spending, but will no longer be spending at a certain time in the future, and add freed up money to the budget.

The most common examples of which would be the costs of children's activities or private schools. Very often there is a high cost of sports or other activities that will no longer occur when high school ends. If the family is spending $5,000 per year on sports or $25,000 a year on private school, we can add that money to the budget once the expense no longer occurs.

We can also add in money from expiring loans such as car loans. Any money that we can find will reduce the amount of money the family needs to add to the budget.

The earlier you start the process, the less it will cost you as your money will have time to grow longer. I wish everyone would start when their children enter grade school, but that rarely happens as extra money is usually not in abundance with young families. Given that, even if you wait until the last minute (kids aged 16-18) this process and the use of IULs can still help you greatly.

Admittedly, these figures we are using here are just estimates. The younger your kids are when you start the process, the more the estimate transforms into a guesstimate. You may end up underestimating the cost, but even if you do, you will be much farther ahead than if you didn't do it, and if you overestimate the cost, you will end up with more money in retirement. Either way, it's a win.

The IUL is best utilized long-term so you reap the rewards of arbitrage for the rest of your life. With that in mind, it's best to pay as much into the policy, for as long as possible, so you only fund not just college, but fund your retirement as well.

Let's take a look at an actual client proposal with a family's real numbers.

Sarah was a single mom with two children, Billy 17 and Gail 14. Sara was 47 and worked as a nurse. Billy wanted to study physical therapy and Gail was considering journalism.

We estimated college costs for both to be $276,000.

We anticipated that together the kids they would receive approximately
- $51,000 in gifting due to financial need,
- $54,000 in student loans, and
- about $30,000 in scholarships.

They would save about $12,000 by Gail taking classes at a local community college during two summers that would transfer over to her primary college. We also added in some other cost-cutting strategies.

We put together a year-by-year college expense budget and determined that we had the following balances that would be paid for through the IUL policy:

Year 3 - $11,830
Year 4 - $11,830
Year 5 - $10,000
Year 6 - $10,062
Year 7 - $ 9,062
Year 8 - $14,062
Year 9 - $14,062

The great news is that, by using an IUL, Sarah would not owe a penny in parent loans when the kids are finished college.

Total budget for the IUL premium was $16,020 per year, which is $1,335 per month.

This is how Sarah helped herself fund that: Of that $1,335 per month premium, Sarah would use $200 a month from the kids' activities that would no longer be needed when they graduate high school. She used $885 from credit card payments, a car loan that would expire shortly, and the balance of $250 was all that was needed to round it out.

She was able to pay the balance of all the college bills for just an extra $250 a month more than she was spending already by redirecting her soon-to-expire debt payments.

As an added bonus, since the vast majority of the IUL premium was from money redirected from old debt, Sarah is able to afford to continue paying the premiums through retirement age which will increase her retirement income from the IUL.

The policy illustration looked like this:

1	2	3	4	5	6	7
						6.25% (2)
EOY Age	End of Year	Premium Outlay	Annual Cash Flow	Annual Outlay	Net Death Benefit	Net Account Value
47	1	16,020	0	16,020	445,249	13,276
48	2	16,020	0	16,020	459,279	27,306
49	3	16,020	11,830	4,190	461,590	29,617
50	4	16,020	11,830	4,190	464,029	32,056
51	5	16,020	10,000	6,020	468,536	36,563
52	6	16,020	10,062	5,958	473,743	41,770
53	7	16,020	9,062	6,958	480,421	48,448
54	8	16,020	14,062	1,958	482,322	50,349
55	9	16,020	14,062	1,958	484,464	52,491
56	10	16,020	0	16,020	501,731	69,758
		160,200	80,908	79,292		
57	11	16,020	0	16,020	521,958	89,985
58	12	16,020	0	16,020	543,517	111,544
59	13	16,020	0	16,020	566,502	134,529
60	14	16,020	0	16,020	591,003	159,030
61	15	16,020	0	16,020	617,116	185,143
62	16	16,020	0	16,020	644,953	212,980
63	17	16,020	0	16,020	674,605	242,632
64	18	16,020	0	16,020	706,183	274,210
65	19	16,020	0	16,020	739,811	307,838
66	20	16,020	0	16,020	775,644	343,671
		320,400	80,908	239,492		
67	21	16,020	0	16,020	813,832	381,859
68	22	16,020	0	16,020	854,525	422,552
69	23^	0	24,000	−24,000	542,276#	427,644
70	24	0	24,000	−24,000	548,574	433,429
71	25	0	24,000	−24,000	555,179	439,974
72	26	0	24,000	−24,000	553,985	447,421
73	27	0	24,000	−24,000	552,138	455,890
74	28	0	24,000	−24,000	549,585	465,517
75	29	0	24,000	−24,000	546,274	476,459
76	30	0	24,000	−24,000	542,156	488,900
		352,440	272,908	79,532		
77	31	0	24,000	−24,000	559,562	502,690
78	32	0	24,000	−24,000	578,664	517,936
79	33	0	24,000	−24,000	599,588	534,748
80	34	0	24,000	−24,000	622,469	553,245
81	35	0	24,000	−24,000	647,445	573,546
82	36	0	24,000	−24,000	674,609	595,732
83	37	0	24,000	−24,000	704,087	619,909
84	38	0	24,000	−24,000	736,045	646,225
85	39	0	24,000	−24,000	770,622	674,797
86	40	0	24,000	−24,000	807,944	705,734
		352,440	512,908	−160,468		
87	41	0	24,000	−24,000	848,239	739,236
88	42	0	24,000	−24,000	891,466	775,251
89	43	0	24,000	−24,000	937,755	813,886
90	44	0	24,000	−24,000	987,215	855,227
91	45	0	24,000	−24,000	1,040,083	899,483
92	46	0	24,000	−24,000	1,068,988	949,108
93	47	0	24,000	−24,000	1,100,592	1,004,720
94	48	0	24,000	−24,000	1,135,517	1,067,323
95	49	0	24,000	−24,000	1,174,892	1,138,483
96	50	0	24,000	−24,000	1,254,260	1,215,389
		352,440	752,908	−400,468		

Column 3 is the premium paid into the policy. That's the $1,335 per month that we budgeted above, which is 16,020 per year.

Sarah will be paying the $16,020 per year premium through age 68 when she plans to retire. The fourth column, Annual Cash Flow, are the loans taken out to pay for college. You can see in years 3-9 they match the anticipated budget exactly.

Remember, Sarah will still be receiving interest on the loans coming out to pay for college, for the rest of her life, whenever the interest credited is higher than her loan cost—which has been most years, historically.

Column 4, Annual Cash Flow, also shows a projected $24,000, tax-free retirement income for the rest of her life.

Column 7 is the cash available. As you can see, there is lots of cash available to Sarah to use for any purpose.

You will also see on the top right corner; these projections are illustrated with an anticipated average performance of 6.25%. The following chart shows the actual historical performance of the index, so there is a strong possibility of even higher returns.

5-Year Average	10.17%
10-Year Average	11.81%
15-Year Average	8.21%
20-Year Average	5.6%

Looking at the projections at age 86, Sarah would have paid in a total of $352,440 over 22 years. She paid off the balance of Billy and Gail's college and created a $24,000 tax-free lifetime retirement income stream totaling $512,908 and had a tax-free, cash balance of $705,734.

Total benefits of $1,218,642 tax-free for a cost of just $352,440.

And…

If Sarah lives longer than age 86, she will continue to increase her income and cash.

And…

She may receive higher amounts if the index performs closer to its historic averages than illustrated.

And…

The vast majority of the money Sarah paid into the policy was from expiring debt, already in her budget. The only extra money she needed was $250 a month.

WOW!

You can pay for college out-of-pocket and kiss the money goodbye, or have the money returned to you in interest for the rest of your life and create a lifetime, tax-free income stream in retirement.

You can replace the "cost of college" with "boat," "wedding," "world travel," even "debt" or the "high cost of aging," and the IUL principle and benefits work the same way, every time.

Seems like a simple and advantageous choice to me.

Financial Tool #3—Stock Market Crash Protection

Here's a mind-bending thought: you can use Indexed Universal Life to help protect your stock market account from running out of money.

We do it by utilizing a buffer strategy that may increase your cash flow and protect your account.

When we look at investment options, there are two basic asset classes: the guaranteed class and the non-guaranteed class, namely the stock market. Both have their advantages and disadvantages.

On the guaranteed side, there are no losses, but returns are not high and we have to pay taxes. But, because the interest is guaranteed, there is good income predictability in retirement.

On the non-guaranteed, stock market side, there are higher returns, but there is high risk and loss potential. You have to pay taxes, but you also have to pay the cost of fees as well, and there is less predictability in your income in retirement.

What if we could combine the best features of these two classes and eliminate the disadvantages?

We can, and I call it the **Hybrid Class**.

In the Hybrid Class, we combine the no-loss advantage of the guaranteed class, and the higher performance of the stock market class, and we add two other big advantages:

1. Elimination of taxes—the income from the Hybrid Class is tax-free

2: Maintain the ability to earn interest on money spent

What I mean by the second point is, when you take money out of your IRA, or any account for that matter, in addition to lowering your balance, you also lose the future investment gain on that money. A dollar spent, or lost to taxes, is a permanent decrease in future returns. With the Hybrid Class, you still earn interest on the money you take out.

If we look at all the benefits: no stock market risk and loss, tax-free income, high single- and double-digit returns, while still earning interest on the money we spend, there is only one financial tool that can do all that. You guessed it, Indexed Universal Life.

The Hybrid concept combines your brokerage account with the benefits of IULs as a buffer strategy to hedge against stock market crashes. The result is that we may increase the amount of money that you will have in retirement and preserve your income.

Let's start by looking at the next chart which is a stress test of a planned retirement income strategy.

1	2	3	4	5	6	7	8
Policy Year	Client Age	Index Year	S&P Rate 2001-2018	Interest Credited	Acccount Value BOY	Withdrawals	Account Value EOY
1	60	2001	-14.54	-290,800	2,000,000	0	1,709,200
2	61	2002	-24.87	-425,078	1,709,200	0	1,284,122
3	62	2003	24.88	319.49	1,284,122	0	1,603,612
4	63	2004	7.49	120.111	1,603,612	0	1,723,722
5	64	2005	1.5	25,856	1,723,722	0	1,749,578
6	65	2006	12.12	212,049	1,749,578	0	1,961,627
7	66	2007	2.03	37,501	1,961,627	114,286	1,884.84
8	67	2008	-39.99	-708,045	1,884,842	114.286	1,062,511
9	68	2009	21.95	208,135	1,062,511	114,286	1,156,361
10	69	2010	11.28	117.546	1,156,361	114,286	1,159,621
11	70	2011	-1.5	-15,680	1,159,621	114.286	1,029,655
12	71	2012	11.91	109.02	1,029,655	114,286	1,024,390
13	72	2013	28.1	255,739	1,024,390	114,286	1,165,843
14	73	2014	9.89	103,999	1,165,843	114,286	1,155,557
15	74	2015	-2.23	-23,220	1,155,557	114,286	1,018,051
16	75	2016	8.04	72,663	1,018,051	114,286	976,428
17	76	2017	17.92	154,496	976.428	114,286	1,016,638
18	77	2018	-7.74	-69,842	1,016,638	114,286	832,510
19	78	2001	-14.54	-104,430	832,510	114,286	613,795
20	79	2002	-24.87	-124,228	613,795	114,286	375,281
21	80	2003	24.88	64,936	375,281	114,286	325,931
22	81	2004	7.49	15,852	325,931	114,286	227,497
23	82	2005	1.5	1,698	227,497	114,286	114,910
24	83	2006	12.12	76	114,910	114,286	700
25	84	2007	2.03	0	700	700	0
26	85	2008	-39.99	0	0	0	0
27	86	2009	21.95	0	0	0	0
28	87	2010	11.28	0	0	0	0
29	88	2011	-1.5	0	0	0	0
30	89	2012	11.91	0	0	0	0
31	90	2013	28.1	0	0	0	0
32	91	2014	9.89	0	0	0	0
33	92	2015	-2.23	0	0	0	0
34	93	2016	8.04	0	0	0	0
35	94	2017	17.92	0	0	0	0
36	95	2018	-7.74	0	0	0	0
					TOTAL WITHDRAWALS	$1,715,333	

Tom and Gail are both age 60. Their account starts with $2 million—third column from the right.

They took out 4% plus taxes $114,286 annually starting at age 66 to give themselves about $80,000 after taxes—Shown in column 7.

A stress test takes the current assets and planned withdrawals and determines what would happen if the historical performance of the stock market repeats itself, as it often does.

In this case, we are using historical returns starting from year 2001—column 4—for a period of 18 years, and repeating that data starting again at year 19. You can use any historical performance data; the concept is the same.

This stress test shows that Tom and Gail would be broke in 25 years—Column 8. Even though they started with $2 million and were only taking $114k per year, the market volatility and crashes devastated their account.

The $114k that they took out during the down years of the stock market cannibalized their principle, eventually eroding it to zero.

The hybrid buffer strategy illuminates the cannibalization of their overall, combined balance, thus maintaining their account balance and income long-term.

The chart to the right is an example of this hybrid buffer strategy combined with the original brokerage account example where Tom and Gail were broke at age 84.

1 2 3   4   5   6   7   8   9   10   11   12   13   14

Hypothetical Illustration   Hypothetical Indexed Universal Life
Male Age 60 Standard Non-Tobacco   Initial Death Benefit: $2,851,704
Historical S&P Performance Years 2001 - 2018, Historical Caps & Loan Rates

Income %:	4.00%	
Portfolio Yr 1:	2,000,000	Tax Bracket: 30%
Level Income:	80,000	Start Year: 7
Cost of Living:	0.0%	

Policy Year	Age	Index Year	Index Return (%)	Annual Premium	Annual Loan	Accumulation Value EOY	Cash Value EOY	Death Benefit EOY	S&P Rate 2001 - 2018 (%)	Withdrawal	Interest Credited	Account Value EOY	Combined Total Withdrawal
1	60	2001	0.00	200,000	-	167,427	167,427	3,019,131	(14.54)	200,000	(261,720)	1,538,280	200,000
2	61	2002	0.00	200,000	60,000	332,490	268,524	3,120,228	(24.87)	200,000	(332,830)	1,005,450	260,000
3	62	2003	14.00	200,000	60,000	564,988	433,472	3,221,210	24.88	200,000	200,396	1,005,846	260,000
4	63	2004	9.00	-	60,000	585,142	382,844	474,726	7.49	0	75,338	1,081,184	60,000
5	64	2005	4.70	-	-	593,810	380,527	464,243	1.50	0	16,218	1,097,401	-
6	65	2006	13.50	-	-	653,522	429,021	514,825	12.12	0	133,005	1,230,406	-
7	66	2007	2.43	-	-	650,869	414,109	492,790	2.03	114,286	22,657	1,138,778	114,286
8	67	2008	0.00	-	80,000	632,717	298,822	352,610	(39.99)	0	683,381	114,286
9	68	2009	14.00	-	-	700,569	350,980	410,646	21.95	114,286	124,916	694,011	114,286
10	69	2010	13.39	-	-	773,720	405,498	470,378	11.28	114,286	65,393	645,118	114,286
11	70	2011	0.00	-	80,000	776,311	306,216	352,149	(1.50)	0	(9,677)	635,442	80,000
12	71	2012	14.00	-	-	887,583	399,766	451,735	11.91	114,286	62,070	583,226	114,286
13	72	2013	13.00	-	-	1,005,778	500,057	555,063	28.10	114,286	131,772	600,712	114,286
14	73	2014	13.00	-	-	1,139,608	610,776	665,746	9.89	114,286	48,108	534,534	114,286
15	74	2015	0.00	-	80,000	1,143,191	511,710	547,530	(2.23)	0	(11,920)	522,614	80,000
16	75	2016	10.78	-	-	1,270,348	613,356	644,024	8.04	114,286	32,830	441,158	114,286
17	76	2017	12.50	-	-	1,433,128	748,213	785,624	17.92	114,286	58,575	385,447	114,286
18	77	2018	0.00	-	80,000	1,437,362	639,939	671,936	(7.74)	0	(29,834)	355,614	80,000
19	78	2001	0.00	-	80,000	1,441,678	501,431	526,503	(14.54)	0	(51,706)	303,908	80,000
20	79	2002	0.00	-	80,000	1,446,051	358,365	376,284	(24.87)	0	(75,582)	228,326	80,000
21	80	2003	14.00	-	-	1,652,581	498,655	523,588	24.88	114,286	28,373	142,413	114,286
22	81	2004	9.00	-	-	1,805,451	586,560	615,888	7.49	114,286	2,107	30,234	114,286
23	82	2005	4.70	-	58,836	1,894,469	547,361	574,729	1.50	30,234	0	0	89,070
24	83	2006	13.50	-	80,000	2,153,897	651,723	684,309	12.12	0	0	0	80,000
25	84	2007	2.43	-	80,000	2,210,076	541,516	568,592	2.03	0	0	0	80,000
26	85	2008	0.00	-	80,000	2,213,652	370,494	389,019	(39.99)	0	0	0	80,000
27	86	2009	14.00	-	80,000	2,525,895	512,349	537,967	21.95	0	0	0	80,000
28	87	2010	13.39	-	80,000	2,865,887	660,755	693,793	11.28	0	0	0	80,000
29	88	2011	0.00	-	80,000	2,867,876	471,230	494,791	(1.50)	0	0	0	80,000
30	89	2012	14.00	-	80,000	3,269,117	699,100	734,055	11.91	0	0	0	80,000
31	90	2013	13.00	-	80,000	3,692,682	945,411	992,681	28.10	0	0	0	80,000
32	91	2014	13.00	-	80,000	4,171,633	1,215,155	1,263,761	9.89	0	0	0	80,000
33	92	2015	0.00	-	80,000	4,172,711	1,023,276	1,053,975	(2.23)	0	0	0	80,000
34	93	2016	10.78	-	80,000	4,624,416	1,264,512	1,289,802	8.04	0	0	0	80,000
35	94	2017	12.50	-	80,000	5,206,980	1,620,879	1,637,088	17.92	0	0	0	80,000
36	95	2018	0.00	-	80,000	5,214,487	1,392,578	1,392,578	(7.74)	0	0	0	80,000
37	96	2001	0.00	-	80,000	5,220,828	1,039,542	1,039,542	(14.54)	0	0	0	80,000
38	97	2002	0.00	-	80,000	5,225,841	682,884	682,884	(24.87)	0	0	0	80,000
39	98	2003	14.00	-	80,000	5,960,962	1,056,467	1,056,467	24.88	0	0	0	80,000
40	99	2004	9.00	-	80,000	6,499,268	1,234,145	1,234,145	7.49	0	0	0	80,000
41	100	2005	4.70	-	80,000	6,804,671	1,169,308	1,169,308	1.50	0	0	0	80,000

This illustration is not NAIC compliant and assumes current charges and index rates of return as indicated.
Actual results may be more or less favorable than those shown.
FOR AGENT USE ONLY

On the right portion of the chart is the same IRA brokerage account that we saw before, but with a couple of changes. We start with same $2 million, but we take three, $200,000 withdrawals to fund the IUL. You can see those in column 5.

On the left is the illustration for the IUL. You can see the three $200,000 premium payments that were transferred from the IRA in column 11.

With a 30% tax rate, we will need to take $60,000 out of the

IUL in years 2, 3 and 4 to pay the taxes. You can see those three withdrawals in column 6. This tax money will come from the IUL as a loan and will not need to be paid out of pocket.

There are taxes due because this example is for an IRA brokerage account, but the Buffer Strategy will work with any type of account.

Going back to the IRA account on the right side of the chart, we are still withdrawing the $114,286 dollars a year, but this time, we are only taking the withdrawals in years when the stock market is positive. (Column 11) There are no withdrawals from the IRA brokerage account in the years that the stock market crashes, so we are not cannibalizing our principle.

Instead, we are taking loans from the IUL in years when the stock market crashes. And you can see those in column 6. We only need $80,000 in annual loans because they are tax-free, unlike the brokerage side where we need to withdraw $114,286 to get $80,000 after taxes.

You can see where there are zero withdrawals on the right from the brokerage account. We have loans (withdrawals) on the left from the IUL, so the client is still getting their annual income, just not from the same account each year.

With the combination of withdrawals and stock market crashes, the brokerage account is dry at age 82.

The client is out of money by age 82 in the brokerage account, but look at the IUL. In addition to all the annual $80,000 tax-free withdrawals to age 100, look at the cash value in column 8. There is still a projected $541,000 in cash value at age 84,

$945,000 at age 90, $1.3 million at age 95, and nearly the same at age 100.

This is how we stop financial plans from failing the stress test. Our Hybrid Buffer strategy can prevent clients from running out of money in later years.

Indexed Universal Life for the win. Again.

Financial Tool #4—Maximizing Wealth Transfer To The Next Generation

This chapter illustrates the benefit of a guarantee insurance policy rather than an IUL, but the concept is too powerful and valuable to leave out of the book.

For many, the purpose of life insurance is for the death benefit to replace future missing income or to pay specific bills such as college or the mortgage. In the case of this book, I showed the value of IULs as a financial tool for growth and income.

It is also a great way to maximize your legacy for the next generation.

You can leave your money in the stock market and your heirs will get what they get, after taxes, depending on the volatility of the market. They may get more than you invested, or if there is a large, untimely stock market crash, they may get far less.

Alternatively, you can use life insurance to multiply their inheritance and give them a guaranteed, tax-free inheritance.

Let's take Mark and Nancy as an example. Both are 60. They planned well, and they have a comfortable retirement income. They have a sum of money they want to leave to their daughter, Rebecca, as an inheritance to pay for college for their grandchildren. We showed them how to use insurance to transfer wealth to the next generations with some great benefits that they did not realize were available.

- The money left to Rebecca will be a multitude higher than what they contribute

- The amount is guaranteed

- It has zero stock market risk

- and it is all tax-free.

Unlike money that you may be saving for your kids and grandchildren in the stock market, perhaps in an IRA, 401(k), or brokerage account, there is no stock market risk with a guaranteed insurance policy. The result is that the life insurance inheritance could be substantially higher than your stock market account.

Let's see how they compare.

Mark and Nancy have $500,000 in an IRA brokerage account that will go to their daughter, Rebecca.

The following chart will compare the historical returns of the market of the $500,000 IRA and a $400,000 policy which is roughly equivalent to the IRA value after taxes.

We are going to use a second-to-die, guaranteed death benefit policy for Mark and Nancy which comes out to about $1.6 million of coverage. I say "about" because the actual coverage will depend on several factors including age, health, carrier choice, etc. I used standard, nonsmoking health rates for this example. Keep in mind, the earlier in life you start the policy, the higher the benefits will be.

I estimated the IRA account performance using the past 23 years of actual historical performance with a 1%

management/mutual fund fee and 35% tax rate to show possible results.

		After 1% Fee	Yield	Balance	After 35% Tax	Tax-Free Life Ins.
2000	-9.10%	-10.10%	-$50,500	$449,500	$292,175	$1,600,000
2001	-11.89%	-12.89%	-$57,941	$391,559	$254,514	$1,600,000
2002	-22.10%	-23.10%	-$90,450	$301,109	$195,721	$1,600,000
2003	28.68%	27.68%	$83,347	$384,456	$249,897	$1,600,000
2004	10.88%	9.88%	$37,984	$422,441	$274,586	$1,600,000
2005	4.91%	3.91%	$16,517	$438,958	$285,323	$1,600,000
2007	5.49%	4.49%	$19,709	$458,667	$298,134	$1,600,000
2008	-37.00%	-38%	-$174,294	$284,374	$184,843	$1,600,000
2009	26.46%	25.46%	$72,402	$356,775	$231,904	$1,600,000
2010	15.06%	14.06%	$50,163	$406,938	$264,510	$1,600,000
2011	2.11%	1.11%	$4,517	$411,455	$267,446	$1,600,000
2012	16%	15.00%	$61,718	$473,173	$307,562	$1,600,000
2013	32.39%	31.39%	$148,529	$621,702	$404,106	$1,600,000
2014	13.69%	12.69%	$78,894	$700,596	$455,387	$1,600,000
2015	1.38%	0.38%	$2,662	$703,258	$457,118	$1,600,000
2016	11.96%	10.96%	$77,077	$780,335	$507,218	$1,600,000
2017	21.83%	20.18%	$157,472	$937,807	$609,575	$1,600,000
2018	-4.38%	-5.38%	-$50,454	$887,353	$576,779	$1,600,000
2019	31.49%	30.49%	$270,554	$1,157,907	$752,639	$1,600,000
2020	18.40%	17.40%	201,476	$1,359,383	$883,599	$1,600,000
2021	28.71%	27.71%	$376,685	$1,736,068	$1,128,444	$1,600,000
2022	-18.11%	-19.11%	-$331,763	$1,404,305	$912,798	$1,600,000

Keep in mind, future stock market losses will further reduce the IRA account.

No matter which way you look at it, life insurance may be a much better platform than the stock market to maximize and transfer wealth to the next generation.

Financial Tool #5—Debt Relief

We love to use our credit cards to buy whatever we need. Lately, we racked up credit card debt to pay for our mortgages, our cars, and even our food.

In 2022, Americans carried an average of $101,915 in total debt for each household, including $5,733 average in credit card debt, according to Motley Fool.[15] And it goes up every year.

The problem comes from the amount of money you pay to service that debt. The interest you pay to the banks and credit card companies is outrageous. It actually is far more than the advertised "APR" (annual percentage rate), because of how the debt gets serviced. For example, a credit card might say its APR is 33 percent. That's very high. But when you look at your credit card statement, the amount being charged for interest is much higher. I've seen it go as high as 58 percent. That is highway robbery, or more to the point, usury. (Usury is when a lender enriches itself unfairly through the practice of making unethical or immoral monetary loans.) [17]

Indexed Universal Life insurance policy loans can be used to pay off debt. It requires that you can do something called "max funding" the policy. Your agent should know how to do this.

The simplicity is this: In order for an insurance policy to remain an insurance policy, there has to be a specific amount of difference between the cash value in the policy and the death benefit the policy is paying out. We've talked about that. It also requires that the policy owner make premium payments for at least five or seven years (depending on your age). In other words, you can't dump all the money you want to put into a policy all at once.

Once you've max-funded the policy, and there is enough cash value built up to fund loans, then have at it. Use loans to pay off the debt. Your debt is paid far faster than if you made minimum payments on the debt—and we all know that is a never-ending cycle of payments designed to keep you in debt and paying the lending institution for the remainder of your life.

Again, this is done with an agent who understands how it works.

It is powerful, possible, and if done right, you have your debt paid off and still have money left for retirement income.

That takes away a lot of the financial stress anyone is experiencing.

Financial Tool #6—Handling the High Cost of Aging

There is a way to use a specific form of IUL to pay for the high cost of aging.

If you've ever had to take care of an elderly parent, you know how expensive everything can get. As your elder becomes less able to care for themselves, the more you pay for items such as incontinence care, trips to the doctors and emergency rooms, even care givers.

Getting old is expensive. People think "Oh, I have enough to make it in retirement," but then when their bodies get old and require more, which means paying more, then that retirement income can quickly get depleted.

There are specific IULs that are designed to cover the high cost of aging. These are different than the "Living Benefits" almost every IUL policy comes with. ("Living benefits" are discussed in the next section.)

With this specific type of IUL, income gets turned on when care is needed, but it can be care in the home, or care in an assisted living facility. Medicare doesn't pay for day-to-day care. It only covers medical bills. Getting old has medical issues involved, obviously, but it's not, in itself, considered a "medical" cost.

The income to help handle these increased costs come from the death benefit and any riders that are attached to the policy. A rider is part of an insurance contract that adds benefits that the policy owner pays extra for. Planning for the high cost of aging is definitely worth paying for. These riders, by the way, cost far less than traditional long-term-care insurance, and they are much more flexible.

Not all life insurance agents know how to write this kind of policy for you, so find one that is knowledgeable and can help you through the process.

Financial Tool #7—Living Benefits

Living benefits allow you to use your death benefit while you are alive if you are sick.

Living benefits can be one of the most helpful parts of a life insurance policy.

As an example, one insurance company offers the following percentages:
Terminal Illness: 75% of the death benefit
Chronic Illness: 50% of the death benefit
Critical Illness: 25% of the death benefit

This means that if you get a critical illness, like cancer, you can let your insurance company know and you can receive 25% of the death benefit, upfront, no penalty.

The living benefits allow you to take a portion of your death benefits if you have a terminal, chronic or critical illness. The exact definition of which and the percentage of your death benefits that you can receive will vary by the insurance carrier.

In addition to death benefits, contemporary insurance policies offer living benefits which allow you to use your death benefits while you are alive if you are sick. Available for both temporary (term) and permanent cash-value life insurance, living benefits may be part of the standard policy or offered as a rider.

These benefits can be extremely valuable if you do get sick. When a serious illness occurs, often the sick person cannot work or has to reduce working hours which will reduce or eliminate income. Copays and medical expenses not covered by insurance add up quickly as well, and if serious enough, the spouse may have to take time off work to take care of the infirmed.

The living benefits in an IUL can be used to pay for medical care, hospice or nursing home care, in-home caretakers, or simply living expenses. They can work on their own or in conjunction with that special kind of IUL I talked about in the previous section.

Bankruptcy Protection
Medical bills are reported to be the number-one cause of US bankruptcies. One study has claimed that 62.1% of bankruptcies were caused by medical issues.[18]

Another claims that over two million people are adversely affected by their medical expenses. The living benefits can alleviate these bills.

Nursing Care
All too often, people do not purchase Long Term Care policies. In fact, the vast majority of people that I talk to do not, and it is surprising as there is a 70% chance that the average 65-year-old will need long-term care services, according to the US Department of Health and Human Services.

Obviously, the cost of nursing home care is extremely high and can drain your assets quickly.

Long Term Care riders are offered by with policies that allows you to use your death benefit while you are alive to cover the cost of nursing home fees and assisted living costs.

One of the uses of insurance policies can be to leverage the cost of long-term care. The living benefits you receive can be multiples of your premium, which would dramatically reduce your out-of-pocket expenses.

Living benefits can help you pay your medical bills, maintain your lifestyle during illness, and prevent bankruptcy. Don't underestimate their value.

Keep in mind that taking advantage of the living benefits does reduce, or may even replace, your death benefit, so be sure that you have your agent help you understand exactly how it works with your policy.

PART 7
Conclusion

17 Where to Buy Indexed Universal Life

While Indexed Universal Life is a life insurance policy, its prime purpose is financial planning. It is not mainly for a death benefit like other life insurance policies.

IULs are not cookie-cutter-type policies. You can't buy them online like car insurance or term insurance.

IULs need to be properly constructed; they need to be designed to match your specific goals and needs.

As such, you should work with an experienced financial specialist, not a general insurance agent. While all licensed insurance agents can sell them, the vast majority of general insurance agents do not understand financial planning and do not truly understand IULs.

Case in point: My three specialties are retirement and financial planning, business planning and college planning. While those may seem like an odd combination, they are actually all related as we use the identical concepts and financial tools with all three, and yes, that includes an Indexed Universal Life insurance policy.

I worked with this one particular family to put together a college and retirement plan. We carefully determined their budget, projected college costs, anticipated financial grants, scholarships and loans, and constructed a long-term plan that included college costs estimated down to the dollar. We knew how much and when college money would be needed.

The family already had an Indexed Universal Life policy that they were paying into, so all we had to do was slide our budget and plan into their policy. In reviewing the illustration for their existing policy, it was very clear that the insurance agent that they purchased it from had no idea what he/she was doing. There were random withdrawals of various amounts spread out through the life of the policy. There was no rhyme nor reason.

I asked the client the purposes of each of the planned withdrawals. Were they for specific purposes, to pay off certain debts, to pay for planned expenses? They replied that these "planned withdrawals" were "*not for any specific reason, they were what the agent thought we could take out.*"

I can't fathom a better definition of an insurance agent that is not qualified to do financial planning.

After reviewing their current IUL policy, I showed them my IUL plan which had withdrawals (loans) that exactly matched the amounts and dates that were illustrated in my college and retirement plan. In the end, the client opted to use my plan to fund college and retirement and they kept their existing plan as a supplement. Had they not, they never would be able to meet their goals with their current policy.

This is just one example of why you should work with a financial professional who understands and specializes in financial planning, not just a life insurance agent or a generalist.

Over forty insurance companies now offer their version of

Indexed Universal Life. Not all policies are the same. Some have better indexing strategies. Some have amazing life benefits. Some allow you to take out policy loans quicker than others. It's up to your agent to find out what is going to fit you best, and you purchase the policy that is going to give you the benefits you need.

Indexed Universal Life cash-value life insurance is an amazing financial tool. It is also something that you need to take the time to understand so that you can get the greatest benefit.

It will be time well-spent.

Endnotes

[1] Jordan Smith. https://www.thinkadvisor.com/2016/11/16/cash-value-life-insurance-makes-harbaugh-college-footballs-top-paid-coach-2/

[2] https://www.thinkadvisor.com/2016/11/16/cash-value-life-insurance-makes-harbaugh-college-footballs-top-paid-coach-2/

[3] https://www.annuitywatchusa.com/the-evolution-history-of-fixed-index-annuities

[4] "Indexing." White paper provided by ARIA (Advanced Retirement Income Analyzer) January, 2023

[5] https://www.schwab.com/ira/roth-ira/contribution-limits

[6] Average bond rate is the historical Moody's Corporate Bond index, an index of the performance of all bonds given a Aaa rating by Moody's Investors Service. This rate is often used as an alternative to the federal 10-year Treasury Bill as an interest rate indicator.

[7] https://www.investor.gov/financial-tools-calculators/calculators/compound-interest-calculator

[8] https://www.nerdwallet.com/article/investing/how-much-does-a-financial-advisor-cost

[9] https://www.marketwatch.com/picks/she-made-about-15k-last-year-off-my-money-my-financial-adviser-is-making-money-off-the-1-million-i-invested-with-her-even-though-im-losing-money-whats-my-move-8beba359

[10] https://www.atlas-mag.net/en/article/bankruptcy-of-insurance-and-reinsurance-companies-in-the-usa

[11] https://www.FDIC.com

[12] https://www.barrons.com/articles/fdic-bank-insurance-depositors-f7261227 page 48

[13] https://www.forbes.com/sites/kennethkim/2016/09/24/how-much-do-mutual-funds-really-cost/?sh=35d0c994a527

[14] https://www.demos.org/research/retirement-savings-drain-hidden-excessive-costs-401ks

[15] https://www.nerdwallet.com/article/investing/how-much-does-a-financial-advisor-cost

[16] https://www.fool.com/the-ascent/research/average-household-debt

[17] "Usury." Oxford English Dictionary. Oxford University Press. 2012. Retrieved 30 July, 2023..

[18] David U. Himmelstein, et al. "Medical Bankruptcy in the United States, 2007: Results of a National Study," Page 741. Elsevier Inc, 2009.

If you like what you read, reach out to us.
We would love to hear from you.

WEALTH CONCEPTS
—— G R O U P ——

(832) 880-5555

www.WealthConceptsGroup.com

www.ingramcontent.com/pod-product-compliance
Lightning Source LLC
Chambersburg PA
CBHW020207200326
41521CB00005BA/272